Dear Bob

I am p̶_____ _____ you
and I hope these memoirs (and
Isabella Graham's) will enlighten
and inspire you! We are proud +
grateful for their boldness and
pioneering in creating a strong
pathway for children and mothers.
to receive "helpful help" when they
are in crisis through out of home
care and vocational services.!

    Happy Reading!
            Kym Watson, CEO
            Graham Windham

MEMOIRS

OF

MRS. JOANNA BETHUNE.

BY HER SON,

THE REV. GEORGE W. BETHUNE, D.D.

WITH AN APPENDIX,

CONTAINING

EXTRACTS FROM THE WRITINGS OF MRS. BETHUNE.

NEW YORK:

HARPER & BROTHERS, PUBLISHERS,

FRANKLIN SQUARE.

1863.

EDITOR'S NOTE.

ABOUT one year before the Rev. Dr. Bethune went abroad and died, he asked me to aid him in preparing a biographical sketch of his mother. He desired me to read her journals, meditations, recorded prayers and letters, and from them to select such passages as might be thought useful if published as an Appendix to the Memoir. After I had completed the examination, I placed the manuscripts in his hands, with the selected passages marked; and he then wrote the Memoir which is now presented to the reader. It is his last work—a beautiful living tribute by a gifted, affectionate son to his sainted mother. Other works of this eloquent and distinguished scholar, poet, preacher, and orator have been published, but nothing from his pen will be read with greater admiration than this simple memorial of the mother who taught him to speak.

The extracts from the writings of Mrs. Joanna Bethune, which are given as an Appendix to the Memoir, are a rich legacy to the Church. In many respects they are not less valuable and interesting than the remains of her remarkable mother, Mrs. Isabella Graham. They exhibit a life of extraordinary activity, of deep spiritual feeling, and strong faith in the promises of God to parents for their children and children's children.

Extending over a long series of years, these extracts, which might have been continued to fill several volumes, complete the biography written by her son, and show the mother in the midst of her incessant toil for the young: founding the Sunday-school Union system, Infant Schools, the Orphan Asylum, and abounding in every good work, humbly seeking Divine aid in the minutest and most secular duties, and, above all, praying without ceasing for the conversion of her posterity to the latest generation.

Christian ladies will read these pages, and be stimulated and guided in noble self-denying labors for the world around them; and aged women will here find a beautiful example of holy living and dying that will comfort and cheer them in the evening of their days.

The life of the author of this Memoir remains to be written. His death, so sudden and in a far-away country, was a shock and a grief to his friends and the Christian community from which they have not yet recovered; but they will receive with mournful satisfaction these last fruits of his pen, the yearnings of his warm heart for her with whom he is now at rest in glory.

The lines below, addressed some years ago by the Rev. Dr. Bethune to his mother, will give the reader a vivid idea of the tender feeling with which the Memoir is written:

TO MY MOTHER.

My mother! Manhood's anxious brow
    And sterner cares have long been mine,
Yet turn I to thee fondly now,
    As when upon thy bosom's shrine
My infant griefs were gently hush'd to rest,
And thy low-whisper'd prayers my slumber bless'd.

I never call that gentle name,
    My mother! but I am again
E'en as a child; the very same
    That prattled at thy knee; and fain
Would I forget, in momentary joy,
That I no more can be thy happy boy;

The artless boy, to whom thy smile
    Was sunshine, and thy frown sad night
(Though rare that frown, and brief the while
    It veil'd from me thy loving light);
For well-conn'd task, ambition's highest bliss,
To win from thine approving lips a kiss.

I've loved through foreign lands to roam,
    And gazed o'er many a classic scene;
Yet would the thought of that dear home,
    Which once was ours, oft intervene,

And bid me close again my weary eye,
To think of thee and those sweet days gone by.

That pleasant home of fruits and flowers,
    Where by the Hudson's verdant side
My sisters wove their jasmine bowers,
    And he we loved, at eventide,
Would hastening come from distant toil to bless
Thine and his children's radiant happiness.

Alas the change! the rattling car
    On flint-paved streets profanes the spot,
Where o'er the sod we sow'd the Star
    Of Bethlehem and forget-me-not.
Oh, woe to Mammon's desolating reign!
We ne'er shall find on earth a home again.

I've pored o'er many a yellow page
    Of ancient wisdom, and have won,
Perchance, a scholar's name; but sage
    Or bard have never taught thy son
Lessons so dear, so fraught with holy truth,
As those his mother's faith shed on his youth.

If, by the Saviour's grace made meet,
    My God will own my life and love,
Methinks, when singing at His feet,
    Amid the ransom'd throng above,
Thy name upon my glowing lips shall be,
And I will bless that grace for heaven and thee—

For thee and heaven; for thou didst tread
    The way that leads me heavenward, and
My often wayward footsteps led
    In the same path with patient hand :

And when I wander'd far, thy earnest call
Restored my soul from sin's deceitful thrall.

I have been bless'd with other ties—
    Fond ties and true; yet never deem
That I the less thy fondness prize;
    No, mother! in my warmest dream
Of answer'd passion, through this heart of mine
One chord will vibrate to no name but thine.

Mother, thy name is widow.   Well
    I know no love of mine can fill
The waste place of thy heart, or dwell
    Within one sacred recess; still,
Lean on the faithful bosom of thy son,
My parent—thou art mine, my *only* one!

CONTENTS.

CHAPTER I.

PARENTAGE.

CHAPTER II.

SCENES OF CHILDHOOD.

CHAPTER III.

EARLY EDUCATION AND ASSOCIATIONS.

CHAPTER IV.

AN UNFINISHED SKETCH BY HERSELF.

A 2

CHAPTER V.

MRS. ISABELLA GRAHAM'S COUNSELS.

CHAPTER VI.

RETURN TO AMERICA.

CHAPTER VII.

EARLY RELIGIOUS LIFE.

CHAPTER VIII.

PLANS OF USEFULNESS.

CHAPTER IX.

MRS. BETHUNE'S ASSOCIATES.

CHAPTER X.

INTRODUCTION OF SUNDAY-SCHOOLS.

CHAPTER XI.

THE ORPHAN ASYLUM.

CHAPTER XII.

MRS. HOFFMAN AND MRS. STARTIN.

CHAPTER XIII.

MRS. GENERAL HAMILTON.

CHAPTER XIV.

THE SUM OF HER LABORS, AND HER REST.

APPENDIX.

MEMOIRS

OF ·

MRS. JOANNA BETHUNE.

MEMOIRS OF MRS. BETHUNE.

CHAPTER I.

PARENTAGE.

Reasons for Writing.—Death of Contemporaries.—Memories of Isabella Graham.—Entail of Grace.—Pious Parentage.—Dr. Graham, of the British Army.—Fort Niagara.—The "Doctor's Garden."—Birth of Joanna Graham in the Fort.

THE eminent and wide-spread usefulness which God granted to the subject of this memoir has caused a general desire that the history of her life should be written, for the honor of Christ, whom she followed, and the encouragement of His disciples, whom she loved. The duty of complying with this wish of many Christian friends devolves on her only son; and he, asking God's help, gladly undertakes it, though not without fear lest the biographer may be suspected of being biased by his affectionate veneration, and so be less trustworthy in his portraiture of his mother's character and services to God and man. But it is true, on the other hand, that none had better opportunities than he of knowing her daily life in private and public, or of hearing from her own lips the reasons and motives from which she acted. There is also less danger of exaggerated praise, so commonly

the fault in modern religious biography, because, as
will be seen in the following pages, her life was so
full of activity that there will be little room for any
thing besides a detail of facts.   The copious extracts
from her own writings, which are given in the Appendix, will show that, for herself, she depended on
the free sovereign grace of Christ alone, and gave Him
the praise of the good works He had wrought in her
to will and to do of His good pleasure.   It would be
most inconsistent with the spirit of so humble and
devoted a Christian, for one who cherishes her memory, so beautiful with the graces of the Spirit, to over-
charge with personal eulogy a life which derived all
its beauty and strength from the love of Christ shed
abroad in her heart; but it would also be unjust to
that divinest principle of Christianity if the genuine
effects of evangelical faith, as manifested in the life-
long, devoted charities of Mrs. Joanna Bethune, were
allowed to be forgotten, or set forth with less than
actual truth.

The author has occasion for regret that the material and authorities for an accurate and full history
of a life covering a period of nearly a century are
not so abundant as is desirable and was expected.
Mrs. Bethune, though not unwilling that the light of
God, shining in her experience and devotion to His
service, should be made to reflect His glory, was too
busy with her duties for any anxiety respecting her
own credit.   She adopted as an axiom the counsel
she learned from the lips of the seraphic Summerfield,

that " a Christian should never bring his good name home to nurse," and left hers to the care of His providence in whom she believed, solicitous rather for her record on high than the opinions even of Christians here. At the time of her death, all of those with whom she had been associated in the most active and fruitful years of her benevolent enterprise had gone to their rest; and there is not a single living memory which can be found to corroborate the testimony which has been gathered into these pages, from records too scanty, but undoubtedly genuine. For some years before her entrance of heaven, her long and overtasked brain yielded to the infirmity of extreme age, and she was not capable of answering inquiries which would otherwise be made of her respecting facts, incidents, and persons connected with the most important passages of her life. Much, therefore, which her biographer would have delighted to rescue from oblivion is now known only in heaven; and, desirous of recording nothing of which he is not sure, he will resolutely check himself in conjecture, and record what he knows to be true.

It is also well known to the readers of the Life of Mrs. Isabella Graham, and they constitute a large majority of the Christian public, that the instrumentality of Mrs. Bethune was closely connected with that of her eminent mother and her equally devoted husband, Divie Bethune, whose biography, full of praise to God, it is the purpose of the author, by God's leave, to prepare for publication when his present work is completed. Much, therefore, that properly belongs to a life of Mrs. Bethune is now before the public in the Life of Mrs. Graham, or will be when Mr. Bethune's memoir is given to the press. But care will be taken to avoid repetition, as far as is possible, consistently with a due regard to historical truth.

The blessing of the Holy Ghost, which rested on the mind and heart of Mrs. Joanna Bethune from her earliest childhood, out of which sprang her ardent desires, her indefatigable efforts and successful plans for evangelical usefulness, are striking proofs of God's faithfulness in His covenant to bestow His grace upon the children of His faithful servants unto the third and fourth generations. She received the entail of religion through a line of pious ancestors even longer than that specified in the promise.

The parents of her mother, Mrs. Graham, Mr. John and Mrs. Janet Marshall, were both pious, Mrs. Marshall's father having been an approved elder of the Scottish Secession Church, which he joined with the Erskines (Ralph and Ebenezer); and the traditions of the family carry the strain of sanctified blood farther back than records or memory of names enable us to reach. The same care of God, preparatory to the life designed for her, will be seen throughout her early history and peculiar training, as described in the following pages.

Joanna was the second daughter of Dr. John and Isabella Graham. Dr. Graham was a widower, with two sons, at the time of his marriage to Isabella, both of his sons afterward becoming distinguished in the British army; one of them, Samuel, after a career of honorable valor, attaining the high rank of general, and being rewarded with the posts of Inspector General of the forces in Scotland and Governor of the Royal Castle of Stirling, where he resided for many years. The other brother was arrested in his military career by receiving a shot through his body at the siege of Charleston, S. C., although he survived his wound, and subsequently married a lady of that state.

Dr. Graham, on thus beginning life anew, cherished a plan of settling in America, somewhere along the line of the Mohawk River, and was glad to relinquish his private and not unremunerative practice in Paisley for an appointment as surgeon in the 60th regiment (Royal Americans), British army, which was stationed in Canada, hoping, should he still desire to make his permanent home in the colony of New York, to dispose of his commission. This somewhat vague and not well-digested plan was the first leading of Providence toward the establishment of Mrs. Graham and her descendants in America.

Within a twelvemonth after reaching Canada Dr. Graham was ordered to join the second battalion of his regiment in Fort Niagara, a strongly fortified post on the right bank of the Niagara River, just where it enters Lake Ontario, founded as early as 1736. The fort has been greatly enlarged, improved, and strengthened since it passed into the hands of the United States, presenting a grand and picturesque

view to the observer from the water or the opposite
shore; but the officers' quarters still remain, only
slightly altered from their original structure. Traditions of the 60th linger about the ramparts, and
until within a few years the site of " the doctor's garden," where Dr. Graham amused his leisure hours,
was pointed out in a peach orchard, afterward planted. Subsequently, we are told, the land, undermined
by the storm-river waves of " wild Ontario," slid into
the lake. The reader is presented with two views;
one of the exterior, from the Canada shore, for which
the author is grateful to the courtesy of the gentle-
manly artist, Captain John Van Clerc, of Lewiston,
Niagara County, N. Y.; the other, a photograph of
the interior, looking west, the discovery of which is
due to the kindness of Captain George Mead, U. S.
Engineers. In the rooms on the ground floor, north
of the entrance of the officers' quarters, Joanna, second daughter of Mrs. Isabella Graham, subsequently
the wife of Divie Bethune, was born, February 1st,
1770.

FORT NIAGARA,

INTERIOR OF FORT NIAGARA.

CHAPTER II.

SCENES OF CHILDHOOD.

The Mother's religious Exercises.—Converse with God.—Religious Studies.—Removal to Antigua.—Toilsome Journey through the Wilderness of New York.—Mrs. Major Brown.—Death of Dr. Graham.—Mrs. Graham goes to Scotland.—Establishes a School for Young Ladies.

THE religious exercises of Mrs. Graham at this period, both before and after the birth of Joanna, were peculiarly deep and decisive. The wild and beautiful scenery about her, combining the flowing river and ocean-like lake with the unbroken virgin forest, through which the roar of the great cataract could be heard, strongly impressed her poetical mind with a sense of the Divine majesty and love. The responsibilities of the young wife and mother, cast upon the care of Providence, far from her native land, her faithful parents, and the pious friends of her youth, and, not least, the difficulty of maintaining her Christian character amid such novel circumstances, and without her accustomed religious privileges, brought her into closer communion with God, making her stronger from consciousness of her entire dependence upon her sympathizing, ever-present Savior. It is true that, in her humility, she condemned herself as low in her religion; but, from her conscientious regard

B

for the Sabbath, her devotional solitudes, her cheerfulness in the discharge of her many domestic cares
amid the trying hinderances of garrison life, her anxious, affectionate desires for her husband's sanctification, her thankful study with him of Doddridge's Rise
and Progress, and her frequent reminiscences in after
life of her days at Niagara, all tend to the conviction
that He who leads his children by ways that they
know not was then educating her for a higher Christian strength and decision of character; nor can we
doubt that her then infant child, unconscious in the
arms of her young Indian nurse, borne among the
flowers of her father's garden, or sleeping under the
blessing of her mother's guardian, prayerful love, received a baptism from the Comforter, invoked by
maternal faith and trust.   He who sanctifies from the
womb can give a blessing in the womb, and sanctify
a mother's travail and nursing at the breast. The
mystery of the new birth will not allow us to understand the ways of blessing God has for the early childhood of the little ones whom believing parents put
into the Master's arms, craving for them the covenant
blessing.

In 1772, the hostilities preceding the war of our Revolution becoming more serious, and it being thought
by the British government to remove the Royal Americans from the danger of sympathy with the Whig
spirit, then rapidly spreading, Dr. Graham's regiment
was ordered to the island of Antigua. The doctor
having gone to New York on an unsuccessful attempt

to sell his commission, that he. might carry out his plan of purchasing a home in Western or Middle New York, Mrs. Graham was obliged to follow him to New York, with her children, assisted by two Indian captive girls which she had, out of kindly motives, received from their savage masters into her family, and who returned her care by a grateful attachment to her and her little ones.   The route which the tender family pursued was by bateau to Oswego, thence over a portage to the Mohawk, somewhere near Oriskany, thence, by alternate canoe voyage and portage (over which the children were carried on the backs of Indians), to Schenectady, and by portage again to the Hudson at Albany.   We have no particular record or *memoranda* of this journey, but how different must it have been through the almost unbroken wilderness, with only canoes to relieve the foot travel, from the means of passage now through the very garden of our beautiful, fertile, and prosperous state. Surely God, who watched over his predestined prophet in the bulrushes of the Nile, guarded and guided that little band through the wilderness and on the stream until they reached New York, the great city which was afterward to be so eminently blessed by the prayers and ministries of Isabella Graham and Joanna Bethune.   While waiting at the sea-port for the sailing of the transport, Mrs. Graham and her young family were treated with most hospitable kindness by many Christian friends, to whom they were introduced by Mrs. Major Brown of the 60th, a daughter of Mr. Vanbrugh Livingston; and made the valuable acquaintance of the Rev. Dr. John Rodgers, of the Presbyterian Church, to whose instructions many years after, on Mrs. Graham's second coming to New York (1789–90), Joanna attributed no small degree of the spiritual benefit she needed at the beginning of her Christian profession.

They sailed for Antigua November, 1772, when it pleased God sorely to chastise Mrs. Graham, first, by the death of her excellent mother, whose letters of affectionate counsel had been of such unspeakable value to her, and, a few months afterward, by the death of Dr. Graham, who died November, 1773, giving the strongest testimony that the blessing which his wife had so earnestly striven and prayed for had been secured through his own apprehending faith on Jesus Christ. Those who have read the memoirs of Mrs. Graham will remember that this was a turning-point of her Christian character. Hitherto she had leaned much on her pious mother in matters of religion, and in affairs of this world on her strong-hearted, affectionate husband. Now, motherless and a widow, sad and in poverty, she looked upon her little fatherless children, and cast herself and them on the covenant care of God alone. After the birth of a son she returned to Scotland (1775), where she found her father, now too aged for the trust from which he had derived his livelihood, living in a little cottage at Cartside, near Paisley. She lived with him in penury for about two years, when, seeking for a better subsistence, she removed to Paisley, and taught a school for small children, which, with her pension as a surgeon's widow, was all her earthly dependence, until her talents as a teacher and her beautiful pious consistency under trial led her constant friend, Mrs. Major Brown (also then in Scotland), to unite several other influential Christian persons to propose that she should open a boarding-school of a high order in Edinburgh (1779), which she taught with great success until her removal to New York in 1789. The reader will observe that from her seventh to her eleventh year she was under the immediate care and instruction of her own mother, whose faculty of teaching the young was the most remarkable of all her distinguished gifts of usefulness, and this, too, during the years when her piety abounded in her deep poverty and sanctified sorrow. Mrs. Bethune was the daughter of a schoolmistress, and her earliest conscious years were spent in her mother's school for young children. The later developments of her intelligent and successful zeal for the religious education of the young prove that the purpose of God concerning her was then in preparation for its fulfillment.

CHAPTER III.

EARLY EDUCATION AND ASSOCIATIONS.

At School.—Her Teachers.—Distinguished Ministers.—Erskine.—
Davidson.—Witherspoon.—A Playmate of Walter Scott.—Lady
Glenorchy; her Biography.

IT would seem from one of her records that about
this time, probably while Mrs. Graham was getting
her school and home in order, Joanna spent nearly a
year in the family of her aunt in Glasgow, when in
1780 she was taken again under her mother's immediate care, participating in the advantages of the excellent school, and the instructions of the eminent
masters whom Mrs. Graham called to her aid. Among
these, Mrs. Bethune retained a strong sense of obliga-
tion to Mr. Scott (author of the once famous book of
rhetorical instruction known as "Scott's Lessons")
and Mr. Butterworth, the first writing-master who
prepared engraved copies for his pupils, and illustrations of the hand holding the pen. To the latter
Mrs. Bethune owed the accomplishment of a peculiarly bold, free, and distinct hand-writing, which she retained as long as she continued to use her pen. To Mr.
Scott she was indebted for a knowledge of the art of
speech and gesture, which made herself the best teacher of elocution the writer of these pages has ever met
with. Thus, at each step of her life, and as her mind

was ripening, did Providence place her in successively higher positions to cultivate her love for education, and ability to advance it on the soundest principles.

But her heavenly Father made yet more striking provision for her religious improvement. Mrs. Graham's respectability of birth—much more, her high intellectual cultivation, and, more than all, her rich endowments of Divine grace shining mildly but unmistakably through her modest virtues, brought around her a considerable circle of friends, some of them conspicuous for rank and professional distinction, as well as unusual piety. Among these were the Rev. Dr. Erskine and the Rev. Dr. Davidson, who, as the Rev. Mr. Randal,* of Glasgow, had been one of her earliest friends while at Paisley, whose ministry she attended while in Edinburgh; the Rev. Dr. Witherspoon, during his visit to Edinburgh (1785), from whose conversation respecting America as a land in which the Church of God was eminently to flourish, Mrs. Graham derived her providential impulses to come with her children to the United States; and other revered clergymen. One of her near neighbors and cherished intimate friends was Mrs. Walter Scott (the mother of the poet), of whose excellent spirit and affectionate kindness Mrs. Bethune often spoke warmly to her children.

It will be interesting here to give some of Mrs. Bethune's reminiscences of young Walter at this time.

* The author believes that this change of name was a condition of his inheriting a fortune, but he has no account of it.

Waltie, as he was familiarly called, Mrs. Bethune described as an amiable, kindly lad, who, from his lameness, was not allowed to play with lads of his age, lest he should suffer from their rough sports, and therefore found his playmates among the girls, with whom he was a special favorite. Their playground was an inclosed space or square, to which the families of the houses round resorted (Mrs. Scott and Mrs. Graham being of the number); and here, upon the grass, it was his special delight to get troops of the young ladies to act little dramas of Border history, the main feature of which was a division into two opposing parties (Englishmen and Scots), who made raids into each other's territory across the Border line, and carried off, if successful, bonnets, shawls, and other articles of clothing deposited for the purpose, as booty. So early did his ruling passion show itself.

At another time the young Joanna, with some other young companions, were spending the afternoon at Mrs. Scott's, when there came up a tremendous thunder-storm, in Edinburgh of comparatively rare occurrence, which so alarmed the little girls that they ran to throw themselves on the feather-beds for safety from the electric fluid. The boy Waltie, being of course excluded, shut himself up in his room, and on the reassembling at the tea-table he produced what appeared to his partial auditors some extraordinarily fine verses on the storm. Sir Walter, in his autobiography, alludes to these verses as among his earliest attempts at verse, in which he says he stole all the ideas and a good share of the rhymes from an old magazine. The writer had often heard the story from his mother before the autobiography reached this country. Sir Walter did not wholly forget his early playmate, but in more than one case introduced friends coming to New York to Mrs. Bethune, and there is now in possession of the writer a copy, quarto, of the first edition of the "Lay of the last Minstrel," which was (as his parents told him) ordered to be sent out by the author. Unfortunately, the poet's autograph is not on it as a presentation copy; nor can any one of the several letters be found, owing to an unfortunate scattering of a portion of Mrs. Bethune's papers, which has been the occasion of many similar losses. Mrs. Bethune was so confident of Sir Walter's kindly recollection of her, that she was anxious her son should bear a letter of introduction to him from her; but his visit to Abbotsford could not be paid until after the Wizard of the North had ceased to breathe his mighty spells over an admiring world. It may be added that in Mrs. Bethune's family the full conviction that none other than her early playmate in "Englishmen and Scots" could be the author of "Waverley," antedated many years his own avowal of the anonymous splendor of those unequaled romances, Mrs. Bethune having detected, as she thought, some unmistakable evidences of "Waltie Scott's hand."

But the friend of Mrs. Graham, most beloved and

trusted in, not for her high, noble birth, but great Christian excellence, and who most deserves mention in this Memoir, because of her influence over the heart and life of the young Joanna, was the Right Honorable Wilielma, wife of Lord Viscount Glenorchy, only son of the third earl of Breadalbane, a nobleman of immense wealth and equal distinction. This lady is named here with her aristocratic titles because she was one of the noblest among the few noble whom the Lord of all honor has called to glorious rank among the highest in the kingdom of God. This lady, adorned by every accomplishment of mind and person, admired, and beloved, and courted by the highest circles in which she moved, by right of birth, through her intimacy with the family of Sir Rowland Hill, father of the eminent preacher of that name, and, at that time (1764), resident with his family, but especially Miss Hill, his eldest sister, became, at the age of 24, so decidedly an evangelical Christian that she broke through all the temptations of the world surrounding her, and ever afterward devoted herself to the unwearied activities and self-denial of Christ's true follower. The Life, with Letters and Devotional Papers, of Lady Glenorchy, was edited by the Rev. T. S. Jones, minister of her chapel, Edinburgh; was published, Edinburgh, for William Whyte & Co., there, and Longman, Hurst, Rees, Orme, & Brown, London, in 1822, 8vo, p. 520, and, though not very skillfully executed, constitutes one of the most remarkable and edifying Christian biographies ever given to the world. It is, unhappily, little known in this country, never having been reprinted here, and it is almost lost to the annals of the Church on earth, so that the writer is compelled to exert no little degree of self-denial in making his notice of his brother's early patron and exemplar sufficiently brief for the size of this volume. Suffice it to say, that Lady Glenorchy was one of Whitfield's school of religious doctrine, while her intimate and best-loved friend Darcy, Lady Maxwell, followed the principles of Wesley,* both being divinely accredited as eminent examples of the power which genuine Christian faith exerts over the hearts of Christ's disciples, despite of technical differences of minor doctrine, in enabling them to overcome the world, to purify their hearts, and work by love. Some notice, necessarily brief, of Lady Glenorchy's character and good works, may be found in the Memoirs of Mrs. Graham, revised and edited for the American Tract Society by Mrs. Bethune, and published from her manuscript, and under her close personal supervision, in 1842; where, also, will be found, p. 64–67, an admirable letter from Lady Glenorchy, showing at once her deeply spiritual character, and the faithfulness of her tender friendship for Mrs. Graham. This she also manifested in her kindness to the subject of this Memoir, in receiving her at one time into her own family, and after-

---

* Life of Darcy, Lady Maxwell, of Pollock, etc., etc. By Rev. John Lancaster. New York: Bangs & Mason, for the Methodist Episcopal Church, 2 vols. 12mo, 1822.

ward sending her, liberally furnished with money for her personal expenses and practical exercise of charity, to a French school at Rotterdam, in Holland, that she might acquire the language, and be fitted for greater assistance to her mother in the school. Lady Glenorchy also requested that Mrs. Graham might be sent for to be near her in her last moments, and Mrs. Graham had the mournful satisfaction of closing her eyes, receiving, as a proof of her friend's love, a legacy of £200, which was of great benefit in her then narrow circumstances.

Again the reader is asked to note the peculiar leading of a gracious Providence in training His young handmaiden for those walks of usefulness which, in riper years, she pursued so successfully and devotedly.

CHAPTER IV.

AN UNFINISHED SKETCH BY HERSELF.

Self-examination.—A Retrospect.—Decline of Religion.—Orphan-
age.—Restraints of Childhood.—A Mother's Care.—An Aunt's
Praises.—A Minister's Influence.—Death of a Grandfather.—
Lady Glenorchy and her Household.—Their Habits and Example.
—Goes to a French School in Rotterdam.—Its effect upon her re-
ligious Character.

HER religious history up to this period will be best
given in the words of an unfinished paper written by
herself immediately after her mother's death.

> "New York, Thursday, August 18, 1814.
> "A day set apart by the General Assembly for
> humiliation and prayer.

"Heard Mr. Bogue preach from Zephaniah, i., 12,
latter clause of the verse: 'And punish the men that
are settled on their lees; that say in their heart, The
Lord will not do good, neither will he do evil.' He
mentioned a number of characters who use such language, and what he said was very good, but I thought
that he came short in not speaking more particularly
to Christians. Those who seem to walk before God
with their whole heart, whose lives and conversation
seem void of offense, have most need to search their
hearts. We are apt to be settled upon our lees. We
live in such a day of Gospel light that it is rather re-

spectable than otherwise to be Christians. There are, indeed, those who spend their days in all manner of riot and dissipation; but there are a good number of real believers, of outwardly decent character, that are under no temptation to go out into the world which lieth in wickedness, having so many to keep us in countenance. For my part, with the deepest humiliation and contrition, I would be this day a witness against myself. When I look back on my past life, and all the way by which the Lord my God has led me, I am ashamed and confounded; and were it not that He hath found out a way by which He can be just, yet the justifier of him that believeth, I could not dare to approach Him, but would be compelled to sit down in despair, and never more open my mouth before Him.

"I am this day, in a particular manner, called to mourn and to rejoice. I am now an orphan. 'My father and my mother have forsaken me.' My father I never knew. It pleased God to take him away before I could be sensible of the loss; but for the space of forty years I have been blessed with the most exemplary of mothers. Although she deeply bewailed her unfaithfulness to her children, I can testify to her faithfulness to me in the best things. The nature of her business exposed her to many temptations from which I am freed; but the Sabbath was always a sign between her and her God. I have always been kept from openly breaking the Sabbath.

"I mean not to record here a history of her life, or

even of her last illness, but strictly to call myself to
account for my conduct from my youth until now;
to enumerate the many advantages I have enjoyed,
and then compare my subsequent conduct.

"As long as I can remember, I daily received religious instructions from my mother.   She taught me
to read, and daily made me learn the Shorter Catechism and portions of Scripture.   I recollect, as early
as when eight or nine years old, having something
like religious exercise.   I yielded to my sisters and
others from a principle of religion, and I was so still
and quiet that they used to call me 'the little pigeon.'
But the corruption in me had not been called into exercise.

"I staid eleven months with my aunt in Glasgow.
She was very partial to me, praising me to every
body, and I soon began to think myself a nonsuch.
This taught me a lesson which I desire ever to remember—not to seek the praise of men, and not to
praise my children before their faces.

"In 1780 we removed [to Edinburgh], and for several years I recollect nothing but childish vanity and
folly.   Dr. Davidson, formerly Mr. Randal, conceived
a great regard for me, and was pleased to fix upon
me as a companion for his eldest daughter, who was
extremely volatile.   I went, for a length of time, to
his house every evening, to study my lessons with
Sally, was present at their family worship, and sat in
his pew on the Sabbath.   Many, very many are the
instructions I received from that man of God, and

accordingly I had something like exercise. I remember my ever making conscience of reading God's
Word, and singing His praises, and praying to Him
every day in private.

"In February, 1783, my grandfather died, which
made a considerable impression on my mind. I
prayed and cried to the Lord only to give me the
portion of His people, and I would ask no other. I
prayed that He would hedge me in, and keep me in
a right way; that, if I ever forsook Him, He would
chastise me, only never take His loving-kindness
from me. Often, often have I prayed in this manner,
when my conduct was in direct opposition to my
prayers; but blessed be my God who has answered
my prayers. He has repeatedly chastised me, visiting my transgressions with a rod, and my iniquity
with stripes; nevertheless, His loving-kindness has
He not utterly taken from me, nor suffered His faithfulness to fail.

"About the month of November, 1783, I went to
Barnton [a seat of her ladyship's], four miles from
Edinburgh, to live in the family of my much revered
patroness and exemplary friend, Lady Glenorchy,
where I remained until the summer following. Oh,
what have I not to answer for what I saw in that family. It was, indeed, a little heaven upon earth. Never, before or since, have I seen such exemplary conduct. The family consisted of Lady Glenorchy [now
thirteen years a widow], Lady Harriet [or Henrietta],
Hope [eldest daughter of the Earl of Hopetoun, who

had resided with Lady Glenorchy since the earl, her father's death, 1781, adding, as Lady Glenorchy's biographer says, 'much to the comfort of her life,' from her clear, vigorous, and evangelical spirit], Miss M'Dowall, the chaplain [the Rev. Dr. T. S. Jones], and myself. Lady Glenorchy was in very ill health during the whole of the winter, never getting out to church or any other place except once on the Sabbath, and sometimes not that; yet I never remember seeing a frown on her countenance or hearing her utter a murmuring word. She was even then deprived of her favorite employment, visiting and relieving the poor. But they did not suffer on that account. She had many almoners. My mother was often honored with that office.* In 1783, when there was a great scarcity, she furnished her friends with tickets, receivable at different shops, and commanding necessaries of life for those who were in want. She had a large room, which she called her wardrobe, hung round with coarse but comfortable garments, which had previously furnished work to many persons in the different stages of spinning, weaving, and making up. She likewise kept all kinds of simple medicines by her for the use of the sick. Her mansion was elegant, and her grounds tastefully laid out;† and, like the great, she had two porters' lodges at the gate.

* So, also, as she often told us, was young Joanna herself, whom Lady Glenorchy used, on such occasions, to call her little almoner. It was part of the education she bestowed on her young *protegé*.

† Barnton was sold for £28,000.

Of these she made schoolrooms, two of her pious domestics having charge of them. In one, the poor children were taught to read, and received religious instructions; in the other, the females were taught to
sew, spin, and knit. I was witness to her having
potatoes planted for the poor in her very pleasure-
grounds. But I can not pretend to enumerate the
many good deeds of that excellent lady, and only,
for my own improvement, set down something of
what my eyes saw and my ears heard. During the
week we worked while one read, generally myself.
Our reading was sacred biography, or the experiences
of pious people. On the Sabbath, our reading was
of a deeper character. Lady Glenorchy kept a little
Bible in the pocket of the carriage, and, while driv-
ing to church [usually four miles, to her ladyship's
chapel, which she had built, and supported, in Edin-
burgh], she would give us a text to meditate upon.
Her whole time, talents, and fortune were devoted to
God, and she had no intercourse with the world except it was to promote some good work.*

---

* Lady Glenorchy's biographer, speaking of her at this period,
says, "In the beginning of the month of September, 1783, she, with
her friend Henrietta Hope, returned to Barnton, where she remained
during the following autumn and winter. 'The liberal,' says the
prophet, 'deviseth liberal things;' much had Lady Glenorchy done,
and much had she expended in promoting the cause of benevolence
and the interests of piety; yet, after all, she was not satisfied; she
never thought that she had done enough while there was a possibility
of doing any thing more. Little or nothing did she expend on herself more than was absolutely necessary; yet she contracted even

"I was often much exercised while staying at Barnton, but I as yet only experienced a wish and desire that little in order to be able to do more good. Her economy became great, but it was the economy of piety and benevolence." She herself writes to her intimate friend, Mrs. Baillie Walker (also an intimate friend and counselor of Mrs. Graham), a lady whose strong mind and deeply religious character had been of special benefit to her (Lady Glenorchy), as it was to all brought within the sphere of her influence, August, 1783, from Moffat, where she had accompanied Lady Harriet, when failing health required the drinking of goat's whey, "The Lord has been pleased to visit me by sickness once more, after my having attained to a measure of health I had not known for several years. May I not say, with Job, 'Shall I receive good at the hand of God, and shall I not receive evil also?' He gave me health for a season, and now He has taken it away; blessed be His name, for He doth all things wise. Yes, I am fully persuaded that this very illness is one of the 'all things' that are working together for my good, and my heart freely acquiesces in the dispensation." Again, in her Diary, January 1, 1783, she records, "The Lord has been pleased, most unexpectedly to me, to lengthen out my life to see the beginning of a new year. . . . He crowns me with every blessing of a temporal nature. I also enjoy the means of grace abundantly; but, alas! how unworthy do I feel myself to be of such favors. How ungrateful, careless, negligent, and forgetful of my best friend and benefactor. I stand astonished at the goodness of God, and at my own total unworthiness. Oh that I had a heart and tongue to praise Him, and power to speed forth to others the grace of God by a holy and useful walk and conversation! May I this year increase in faith, love, and power in my soul, that God may be glorified in me and by me. Let my soul live, and it shall praise Thee! Amen, and Amen!" Again, January 26th, "For some days past I have had more liberty in prayer, and more comfort in secret duties than usual, particularly in the morning; and sometimes in the night, when I awake, I have been constrained to praise Him for all His mercies. I have had several instances of His answering my prayers for spiritual blessings, and find my mind led

to become a follower of Jesus, and never pretended
to think that I had already attained to a right knowledge of Him.   The doctrine of election puzzled me;
and, besides, by frequently hearing the Methodists, I
expected to experience some sudden change, nay,
even that all my evil inclinations would be at once
done away, and that ever after I should feel entirely
free from sin.

"Lady Glenorchy, out of her great benevolence,
and warm friendship for my mother, in order to fit
me to assist her in the school, sent me, at her own
expense, to a French school in Rotterdam; and, that
I might have opportunity for my private devotions,
paid for a room private to myself, a privilege of which
I was defrauded.   She also gave me ten guineas for
pocket-money, enjoining it upon me never to see distress without relieving it.   I parted from this dear lady
in 1784, and never saw her again.   When I arrived
in Rotterdam, I found myself without a pious friend.

out to trust and look for yet greater blessings than any I have hitherto experienced.   I want to be more habitually spiritually-minded,
and to live under a constant sense of His presence; to act, as in His
sight, with a single eye to His glory.   My soul longs for the mind
which was in Christ.   O Lord, grant me all thou art willing to bestow on me, and then take me to thyself, that I may behold thy
glory without a veil."   Such was the heavenly and heaven-desiring
frame of Lady Glenorchy's mind during the time when young Joanna Graham, then just passing out of her girlhood, had the inestimable privilege of living under her affectionate care, and of being
the subject of her prayers.   The subsequent career of Mrs. Bethune
will develop the degree in which her heart, judgment, and method of
pious action were affected by what she saw and heard at Barnton.

On the Sabbath the girls amused themselves more than on week-days, and although I understood that there were many pious people in the place, it was not my lot to meet them. I was dreadfully afraid, and cried earnestly to the Lord to preserve me from breaking the Sabbath as I saw others do. Indeed, I never in my whole life prayed more earnestly than I did when first in Rotterdam; but, by degrees, I became accustomed to the state of things around me. The society of young people, and the example of careless ministers" [assistants in the school, and perhaps others, who exhibited the deplorably lax notions on the Sabbath prevalent among churches on the Continent], "soon wore off my serious impressions; and although I do not recollect deliberate joining in any game or amusement on the Sabbath, yet idle conversation and laughing occupied too great a part of the holy day. By the time I was ready to return home, my affections were much turned from serious things, and I do not recollect much exercise for some years, but much, much folly of heart and life.*

"The year 1786 I must now recollect with great

---

* Truth requires the biographer to say that, notwithstanding the many disadvantages under which she labored at this worldly-minded school, Mrs. Bethune often spoke with pleasant reminiscence of some parts of the French service in the church the school attended, and also of the weekly visits of a little man in half clerical costume, the catechist (*catechiseermeester*), an officer in the Reformed Churches who, according to their praiseworthy custom, came to hear the pupils say their Catechism, etc.

sorrow; for not only was I cold and indifferent as to religion, but I gave up praying altogether. Indeed, I was afraid to pray; but the Lord had purposes of mercy concerning me." Here the narrative ends.

Nothing of interest concerning Joanna's life is recorded from this time until July, 1789. It is probable that she assisted to some degree in teaching her mother's pupils, but not so as to hinder her own thorough education.

CHAPTER V.

MRS. ISABELLA GRAHAM'S COUNSELS.

Letter to a Daughter at School.—Love of Enjoyment.—Discontent.
—Great Opportunities.—Pleasures of Home.—Mother's Cares.—
Advantages of Education.—Gratitude.

THE following is one of several letters of Mrs.
Graham to her daughter, and will not be without
interest. It would seem that Joanna was, for some
good reason, to be transferred from the school which
she had entered at first, and had expressed some im-
patience:

"Edinburgh, May 3, 1785.

"To Miss Jacky* Graham, at Madame Marc's
"Boarding-school, Rotterdam:

"MY DEAR GIRL,—Before I begin this letter, I must
put you in remembrance of what I have often told
you, that it is no strange thing for either youth or
age to need friendly caution, or even reproof; and
that if ever you find yourself for any length of time
without it, it is not because you do not need it, but
because you have no friend near, or none that is
faithful, or none with penetration, or none who strictly observes your actions; for inspired wisdom itself has said, that folly is bound up in the heart of
youth, and needs the rod of correction to drive it

* The pet name for *Joanna*.

out. I have never, as you know, dealt much in cor-rection, but have ever labored to rectify the judg-ment, the heart, and the passions. Now, my love, I have no crime to charge you with, nor even any real fault; I only think that you are too much under the influence of self-will—no, I can not say that either; I rather say, *the love of present enjoyment.* You would, in every letter, leave all the advantages you have for improving yourself, and return, more than satisfied, to your mother's house. You would forego all the advantages of the future for a year's present enjoy-ment. I should be vexed and grieved if any of my children could be so happy absent from me as with me. I even wish them to prefer home to every other situation.

"That you are more reconciled to your present situation is because you have found another *home—* other kind friends, who have become objects of your esteem and affection. This, too, is good. You owe them, and every other blessing, to the great Fountain of love, who has the hearts of all in His hand, and opens or shuts them at his pleasure. You owe to them gratitude—you owe them love. You may without offense, nay, it is ever your duty, to enjoy them while with them. But, my dear Jacky, as it was your duty to leave your mother's house, and go to Holland a stranger and unacquainted, so it is your duty to leave your second home, and become more a stranger and unknown; and that with your will heartily, though it should be with painful feelings.

God is every where, and can ever raise up friends
for you wherever He, in His providence, calls you.
Does my Jacky reflect when she says, 'I was born
to suffer; it is hard to be tossed about in this manner?' Does she not, at such times, forget that all
this is for her own improvement, and that God has,
in a very remarkable manner, provided the means
of such improvement, for your mother had it not?
What would poor Juliet ——, and thousands of others, give for your opportunities? Yes, your own
sister Jess would at present esteem it a happiness, though, I make no doubt, she would feel as
you feel, and say as you say, or, perhaps, be even
more impatient, if actually in the same circumstances. Still, in the view of sober reason, your advantages are greater than theirs who are at home,
and your situation comfortable at the same time.
Turn back your views to your mother's situation:
left a widow, with four of you, in a distant country,
with scarcely so much in hand as to carry her and
her orphans to her native land. Next, view our cottage [at Cartside]—no doubt it was the cottage of
innocence, simplicity, and happiness, though of poverty—and even from that we were shut out with
but a poor £16 a year to depend upon, and the eldest of my children scarcely eight years of age. What
could be our prospects at that time? Either sitting
from six in the morning till ten at night sprigging
muslin, or some such work, or going out to common
service? Many late, many anxious nights your

C

mother had at that time; and she who had ever
lived a life of ease and plenty in the lap of indul-
gence, loving and beloved—her company courted—
her conduct copied—the seeming favorite of all who
knew her—yet brought so low as to be obliged to
part with her last servant, and do her own house-
work; and, what was worse, be neglected by those
who were formerly my intimates, some of whom had
esteemed my friendship an honor. What were my
prospects then? Yet, Jac, think what the Lord has
done for us since that time, and you in particular.
Relations, afraid of being entangled in our difficulties,
kept at a distance; but the Lord opened the hearts
of strangers to countenance me and find business for
me. Yet what would even this have done for me
had I been without education? I have had the happiness of seeing my children possess all the means
of a most liberal education, and enjoying a circle of
worthy friends and acquaintances. If I am taken
away before they be of age to carry on the present
school, or should the business fail, though I can not
leave them in abundance, I should leave them with
such acquisitions and talents as will render them
blessings to, not burdens on society, dependent
though they will be on character, behavior, and
their own exertions for a livelihood. If they be-
have with propriety wherever they are, they will be
respected, and entitled to keep company with people
of education, and never need be in want of a home
gained by their accomplishments. Bless the Lord

with me, my dear, and forget not all His benefits, who is, in truth, the widow's help, the orphan's stay, and the stranger's shield."

Under such faithful and affectionate training she remained until the family left Scotland for the United States.

CHAPTER VI.

RETURN TO AMERICA.

Dr. Graham's Views of Settling in America.—Mrs. Graham's Plans.
—Christian Friends.—Dr. Witherspoon.—Mrs. Graham and Fam-
ily arrive in New York.—Reception.—Success.—Mrs. Graham's
School and Patrons.

THE reader will remember that Dr. Graham's main
motive in getting commissioned to serve in America
was the hope of finding there, with his young wife's father and mother, a rural agricultural home. Though
the idea, as he entertained it, like similar projects of
many others, was rather romantic than wise, the impression remained deep on the mind and heart of
Mrs. Graham; and though compelled by adverse circumstances, and the state of war in this country at
the time of her widowhood, to return to Scotland,
she seems never to have lost the desire of establishing her family in the land where she had spent the
happiest years of her womanhood, and where her
daughters were born. It is even more than probable
that she accepted the opening made for her in Edinburgh under the design of thoroughly educating her
girls for a similar enterprise in New York. Her
friend, Mrs. Major Brown, who had come to Scotland
with her husband, was, as we have stated, a native of
New York, being the daughter of Mr. Vanbrugh Liv-

ingston, a distinguished member of that opulent family, even then occupying a high social position in the new state, as it had from an early day in the colony. Doubtless the conversation of these ladies was often turned, in their confidential moments, to the city, which soon gave strong promise of its future prosperity and influence. The great kindness of the Christian friends who ministered to Mrs. Graham in 1772, when on her way to Antigua, and most probably the correspondence of Mrs. Brown with her relatives there, were not without the effect of keeping alive Mrs. Graham's predilections and desires. Thus did Providence prepare her mind to listen favorably to the suggestions of that eminent divine and distinguished patriot, the Rev. Dr. Witherspoon, who paid a visit to his native land, and was intimate with the circle of Mrs. Graham's friends. Devoted to the highest welfare of his adopted country, which he served so well, and especially to the religious and general education of its youth, on whose proper education for their duties so much of the prosperity of the young republic depended, Dr. Witherspoon, the President of Princeton College, readily perceived how able a coadjutant such a woman as Mrs. Graham, with such a family, would be to him, and he spared no pains to persuade her that in New York she would find a sphere for her zeal in advancing her usefulness and the glory of God, especially as it was his deep conviction that in this land the Church of God would eminently flourish, and become a praise in the whole

earth.   It is not surprising, therefore, that in the summer of 1789 she broke up her flourishing school in
Edinburgh, and, tearing herself away from her faithful and beloved friends, who had been her stay and
comfort, she came, after having received earnest invi-
tations from most respectable sources, to New York,
in September of that year.   She was received with
great deference and kindness by the best people in
the city.   This was partly secured to her by the regard of the friends she had gained in 1772, a number
of whom were still living; also by the distinguished
introductions she was favored with from divines and
others in Scotland, as well as from Dr. Witherspoon,
who spared no efforts to open for her the best opportunities which, from the combination of his high political as well as social and literary eminence, he was
well able to accomplish; more than all, from the deep
anxiety of the most influential families in New York,
and throughout the country, to secure for their daughters such an instructress as Mrs. Graham's friends cer-
tified her to be.

Mrs. Graham's school, which she speedily opened
under such favorable auspices, was, it is believed, the
first, and for many years the only school in the States
where young ladies could obtain a thorough and elegant education, with the yet higher advantages of
sound Christian training.   The Congress of the United
States then held its sittings in New York, where, con-
sequently, the President (General Washington), the
heads of departments, and the members of both

houses resided, at least for a considerable part of the year. Next to the power of religion, the city could scarcely have received, especially for the younger women, a greater or more needed blessing than such a school as Mrs. Graham's. Hence we find the excellent Bishop Moore, of the Episcopal Church, the Rev. Dr. Rodgers, of the Presbyterian, the clergy of the Dutch Church, and others high in the confidence of the Christian community, united in encouraging Mrs. Graham to undertake a school of the highest order, which was soon filled to its utmost capacity, and fully employed the talents and time of her two daughters, Joanna and Isabella (afterward Mrs. Andrew Smith, who died in March, 1860, in Glasgow, Scotland, at the house of her daughter, the widow of Mr. John Brydon, a gentleman of modest, but very great worth), Jessy, the eldest, having married Mr. Hay Stevenson soon after their arrival.

CHAPTER VII.

EARLY RELIGIOUS LIFE.

Joanna Graham a Teacher.—Marries Divie Bethune, Esq.—Her own Record of Religious Experience.—Remarkable Conflicts.—Darkness.—Delirium.—Restoration to Health, Peace, and Happiness.

JOANNA had now reached adult womanhood, and her early developed love of education led her to devote her ripe, cultivated powers to the benefit of the pupils, including, as has been said, the daughters of many of the most distinguished families in the land, at a period when the best influence of instructed and religious mothers over the future rulers of the young republic was so especially needed. In the long lapse of time, the most of Mrs. Graham's pupils have passed away from earth; but Mrs. Bethune's family, in earlier days, have been often delighted to hear from ladies of the highest and most important positions the warmest expressions of grateful admiration for Joanna and Isabella Graham, who were at once their teachers, their examples, and friends. Thus was occasioned the wide and commanding influence which Mrs. Bethune had over the best female minds, and of the highest social standing with reference to the various schemes of usefulness she was called by Providence to inaugurate, organize, and establish.

Joanna continued to assist her mother until 1795, when she was married to Mr. Divie Bethune, a gentleman characterized, like herself, by ardent piety, a strong, cultivated mind, sound doctrinal views, great desire and great aptness for usefulness, so that their union, while it increased their personal and domestic happiness, favored yet more their zeal and faculties for doing good. For twenty-nine years Mr. and Mrs. Bethune walked hand in hand through the private and social duties of the Christian life, encouraging and assisting each other in successive plans of religious and philanthropic exertion, which have been, some of them for many years, and are not less at present, abounding streams of usefulness in this city, throughout the land, and in many foreign parts, making glad the City of our God.

Mrs. Bethune's personal narrative during this period, from 1789 to 1795, in the manuscript already referred to, and from which large extracts have already been made, is so full of interest that I transcribe it almost *verbatim*.

"We left Scotland in 1789, and, after passing through a fiery trial, arrived in New York September 8th of that year. The Lord greatly blessed us, and gave us favor in the eyes of this people. He also provided for us Christian friends, Rev. Dr. Rodgers, Dr. Mason [the elder], and Mr. Mason, John M. Mason [afterward the eminent Dr.], dear Mr. Chrystie, and others. The first winter I was confined entirely to the house with rheumatism in my head,

while my sisters were visiting about; yet it pleased
the Lord to make this trial a blessing to me. In my
retirement and frequent solitude I remembered my
evil ways, and loathed myself for my sins in God's
sight. I read Doddridge's Rise and Progress through,
prayed over all the prayers in it, and, in the spring
of 1790, began to attain some degree of comfort. Dr.
Mason often called and spoke to us in the most affectionate manner, never failing to melt me into tears.
My mother saw that I was deeply exercised, and persuaded me to call on Dr. M., who seemed pleased with
my exercises, and advised me to come forward to the
sacramental table. I think that I was sincere, and
desired with my whole heart to belong to the Lord;
but I had not yet attained sufficient assurance. Had
I continued to follow on to know the Lord, no doubt
I should have attained to that grace; but alas! alas!
like the Israelites who longed after the flesh-pots of
Egypt, I imagined that I might indulge in what the
world calls innocent amusements. I did not go to the
play-houses or other public places of diversion, except occasionally to a concert; but I attended private
dancing parties, and was too fond of gay, thoughtless
people, and, in consequence, I was miserable. I was
trying to serve God and Mammon. Often, when in
company, I used to look round me and wonder if
there were any there besides my sister and myself
who professed to be followers of the meek and lowly
Jesus, to take up the cross and go after Him through
evil as well as through good report. I had often

convictions that I ought to come out from the world entirely, but had not the resolution. By degrees I discovered the emptiness of all created enjoyments, and for a considerable time continued to be unhappy in worldly company. I was often tempted to stay away from the Lord's table. I dreaded death. I knew that I was acting contrary to the law of God, and feared that I should be cast out at last. I was even tempted to wish I had never heard the Gospel in my youth, that it might make a stronger impression on my mind as if I heard it for the first time. I thought that I had sinned away my day of grace, and had become hardened under the droppings of the sanctuary. I prayed the Lord to afflict me, to do any thing to me so that I might attain comfort at last. But still I did not cut with the world—I did not give Him my whole heart. In 1793 I formed an acquaintance with an Irish gentleman, who paid me great attention. I was pleased with him, for he was well read, especially in poetry, of which I was then passionately fond. I gave him no encouragement except my company, which I now think was wrong. He often said that I had but one fault, which was being too religious. Alas! I thought myself any thing but that. One Sabbath evening he persuaded the maid to let him into the room where we generally sat, and on my coming in from attending church the third time that day, I found him there. He immediately began to talk of the folly of going so often to church, and that he hoped to get me where the sound of the church bell was never heard. I shrank from him with horror, and from that time I determined not only to break with him, but also never to give my company to any man connected with whom I might be exposed to breaking the Sabbath, or to temptation which I was convinced I could not resist. I might have formed a matrimonial connection with a wealthy merchant, but was preserved; or, rather, Providence so ordered circumstances that he who afterward became my beloved husband was the only one who actually proposed to me, which was rather unexpected, as, although he was a frequent visitor and highly esteemed, I knew not at the time of the strong attachment he felt for unworthy me. At the communion table, after my dismissal of my Irish lover, I made a solemn vow that I would never connect myself in marriage with one who was not a decided Christian in profession and practice, but would rather lead a single life.

"During the following winter, say 1793–94, I occasionally went to private parties, and we had sometimes dancing in our house; but I had no relish for such enjoyments. Mr. Bethune told us of Dr. Rodgers's and Dr. Livingston's lectures on Wednesday and Thursday evenings, and also the prayer-meeting on Tuesday evenings, maintained by the Wall Street Church people in their lecture-room on Nassau Street, near Wall (west side). My sister and myself resolved to attend them, which we did. My religious exercises of mind were deepened, but still I was without assurance. I no longer hungered and thirsted after the world; its pleasures were husks and chaff in my mouth, and bitterness in retrospection; but still I did not altogether decline invitation, partly because my sister wished to go, partly because I knew not what excuse to make, and dreaded the laugh of the world. Toward the middle of the winter I spoke again to my sister, and we agreed to set apart Wednesday and Thursday evenings for attending the lectures of Drs. Livingston and Rodgers, and when invited out on those evenings to answer we 'were engaged.' The very next Thursday we received an invitation from one of our former boarding scholars to an evening party given as a farewell to New York. Upon our returning an answer that we were engaged, she called herself to see if we could not break the engagement, or if we could not go to tea, to come to her as late even as 9 o'clock. To this my sister consented. Never, never shall I forget the lecture of that evening. Dr. Rodgers's subject was the 38th question and answer of the Shorter Catechism: 'What benefits do believers receive from Christ at the resurrection?' *Ans.* 'At the resurrection, believers, being raised up in glory, shall be openly acknowledged and acquitted in the day of judgment, and made perfectly blessed in the full enjoying of God to all eternity.' While the good old doctor explained and commented, I inwardly prayed that I might be among that happy number, and felt such a solemnity on my mind that the world and every thing in it seemed like nothing,

and less than nothing. I loathed myself in the sight
of God, and asked only one thing, that I might be indeed of the happy number of those described. When
coming out of the lecture-room, I asked my sister if,
after such a solemn season, she could go to a worldly
party? 'No,' she replied; 'not for the world.' . . .
That evening Dr. Rodgers gave notice that, as he
should necessarily be absent from the city, there
would be no lecture on the following Thursday.
Next day, or soon after, we received an invitation to
a party for that evening; and, as there was to be no
lecture, we could not with truth say that we were engaged, and we accepted. I determined to keep it out
of my mind as much as possible, and made no addi-
tional preparation in dress. I spent some time in
prayer to God before I went, earnestly beseeching
Him that, if I was doing wrong, He would make a
way of escape for me. My mind was very solemn
all the evening, and, as I recollect, the master of the
house rallied me on being religious, but gave a testimony to the character of Dr. Mason as being 'an
honest priest;' that is, consistent in his walk and conversation with what he preached. 'Alas!' thought
I, 'am I consistent?' and, looking on the thoughtless
crowd flitting in the dance to 'the sound of the viol,'
I said to myself, 'Are these the persons who will receive the blessings of eternal life as Dr. Rodgers described them? are these suitable companions for me,
if I am a follower of the Lamb?' I danced but little, and I believe that my serious air and listless man-

ner gained me no favor with my partners. As we were going down stairs to supper, I lifted up my heart in prayer that I might never again be found in such a scene. . . . Judge how I was shocked when the master of the house, standing at the foot of the table, said, 'Ladies and gentlemen, I said grace coming down stairs, to save time;' at which the company laughed heartily. I almost feared to look around, and feared lest the earth should open and swallow us up; but I thought myself the most guilty of all, for I knew better, had been trained in the nurture of the Lord from my youth up, nay, had professed at the table of the Lord to renounce the pomps and vanities of this world. I felt ill; and, declining all entreaties to return to the dancing-room, we ordered our sleigh and went home. I flew to my chamber, and, throwing myself with all my feathers, and flowers, and furbelows on the floor, was dumb before the Lord. I groaned, and wept, and loathed myself under His eyes, who now seemed to leave me in despair. All I remember of my prayer was that I might never be found in the seat of the scorner again. Rising from the floor, I opened my Bible, if perchance the Lord would send me some comfort; but here I was met with these words, the first that presented themselves: 'Woe unto them that are at ease in Zion!' (Amos, vi., 1); and, reading on through the prophecies, I could only find woes denounced against myself; but one thing I resolved, to give myself no rest, night or day, until I found grace in believing; for I felt that the

world could never fill the aching void I felt. If I
were never made happy in believing, I could not and
would not look for happiness in the creature. I determined to fast, and pray, and read; and then surely the Lord would accept me. I borrowed Pilgrim's
Progress, with Scott's notes, and read it with prayer;
but I could not get out of the 'Slough of Despond'
with Christian. I struggled, indeed, toward the side
nearest the wicket gate; but Sinai's fires glared on
me, and I could not see the Redeemer's smiling face.
Satan constantly suggested that I had sinned away
my day of grace—that I had 'once tasted of the heavenly gift,' but had fallen away, and it was 'impossible
to renew me again unto repentance;' in short, I could
see 'no more sacrifice for sin' for me, but 'a fearful
looking for of judgment and of fiery indignation,
which shall devour the adversary.' In February,
1794, my beloved husband professed his love for me;
and, adverting to his poverty, he talked much of living by faith. Although a professor of Christian faith
before him, I did not understand him. I felt sick of
the world; and, blaming myself for having given encouragement to former admirers whose hopes I disappointed at last, I determined to decline his addresses, and did so. My dear mother, who loved him dear-
ly, was quite angry with me, and declared that I refused him because he was so religious; and added,
'Joanna, if he has asked you in faith, he'll get you in
spite of your teeth!' I said, 'Now, mother, don't go
and pray about it, for I don't expect ever to marry;

and, besides, it would be the height of imprudence to give him encouragement, and make so long an engagement with one who had no prospect of supporting me.' My heart was free, and that I never would give encouragement to any one until I felt a preference for him over every worldly consideration.

"Mr. Bethune continued to visit; and as my mind was every day becoming more and more serious, and his conversation was so heavenly, I soon found that the more earnest I felt to attain assurance and holiness of life, the more he gained on my affections, and in May I consented to wait with him on God for future provision in life. He proved a help-meet to me during a longer season of darkness and doubt which God was pleased to keep me in.

"In May, 1794, we moved from Broadway, near the Battery, to Liberty Street—from a gay neighborhood to one much plainer, and the Lord thus began to answer my prayer, and to fulfill His promise, on which I had laid hold—Ex., xxxviii., 23: 'Neither shall they defile themselves any more with their idols, nor with their detestable things, nor with any of their transgressions; but I will save them out of all their dwelling-places wherein they have sinned, and I will cleanse them; so shall they be my people, and I will be their God.' I could not, at that time, live out of the promises. I hoped against hope. I cried, or tried to say, 'Lord, I believe!' but could adopt only the last part of the verse, 'Help my unbelief.' During all these exercises, I hid them from my

mother and from my dear friend, as I thought that
they would despise me if they knew what a hypo-
crite I was. Often, when Mr. Bethune came in, have
I gone from my knees and reading my Bible to playing and singing, or light conversation, that he might
be blinded to my true feelings—so much so that he
was grieved at my seeming worldly-mindedness, and
prayed much that I might be brought off from the
world. . . . I tried to appear what I professed to be,
a *Christian*, but my conscience accused me of hypoc-
risy. I had all the time a fearful misgiving that,
while I had a name to live, I was still 'dead in trespasses and sins.'

"In August we had our school vacation. My
mother had engaged country lodgings at the Narrows, Long Island, for such of the young ladies as
had no place to go to. She went down with them in
a boat, and Mr. Bethune was to drive me down the
next day in a gig. The day previous to their leaving, Mr. Mason lectured on the parable of the barren
fig-tree in the morning, and applied the subject in the
afternoon. Under this discourse I felt as if he had
said, 'Thou art the woman! For three years hast
thou been a professor, and have brought no fruit!'
I acknowledged it, and assented in my mind to the
justice of God should he cut me down as a cumberer
of the ground. I felt convinced that Mr. Mason had
reference to me, and that his eyes and the eyes of
many in the church were fixed on me, so that I was
obliged to put down my head on the book-board be-

fore me. Mr. Bethune saw how deeply I was exercised, and was much pleased. In the evening we went to hear the Rev. Mr. Pilmer, in Ann Street; and it was so ordered that his subject was peculiarly suitable to my exercises. His text was, 'I will not let Thee go until Thou bless me!' I determined on wrestling in prayer until I found the blessing; but, still, not apprehending Christ as freely offered, without money and without price, I set about establishing a righteousness of my own. I sometimes accused God of injustice and unfaithfulness, as if I had complied with His requisitions, and He had not fulfilled His promise. I literally wrestled through the whole of that night, and rose in the morning to shut myself up to continue wrestling, and, as far as I can remember, I neither ate nor drank till evening. The maid came to the door several times, begging that I would take some food, but I remained, after my severe wrestling and agony, in a kind of torpor, from which I was roused to exertion only by the thought that Mr. Bethune would soon call, and I felt anxious to hide my exercises from him. I rose from the dust, dressed myself, and went down to the parlor to wait for him. Opened the piano and began to play. The song I opened to was from the Woodman, called 'The Sapling Oak.' Here, again, my own case met me; and, what is strange, I seemed to discover a ray of light. The song describes a sapling oak lost in a dell, and thickly surrounded by tangling brakes, which prevented it from growing to maturity. At length the woodman cleaves them away, and,

" ' High, reviving o'er the ground,
The forest monarch lifts his head.'

. . . . Here, thought I, is a representation of myself.
I have been tampering with the world, and its cares,
like thorns, have choked the word, and prevented
my growth in grace. The Lord will, and I prayed
that He would, remove all these ' tangling brakes,'
and cause me, like the oak, to rise above all, and become ' a goodly tree in the house of my God.'

" After I went to the Narrows I continued reading,
and praying, and looking for deliverance. Keeping
still among the promises, I could read nothing but
the Bible. I hated the sound of every thing relating
to this world. I thought every thing sinful except
preparing for eternity. Nothing had charms for me.
Nature, even at her most beautiful season, seemed to
mourn—the whole creation to groan—because of sin.
A poor sailor, that came begging, and used profane
language, made me quite sick, and I shuddered at the
awful thought of the multitudes going down to hell,
and Christians caring for none of them. I wandered
about early in the morning and late in the evening,
bemoaning myself, and wondering at the long-suffering of God in permitting a sinner such as I was to
live. This brought on a severe cold, which landed
me in a fever. One Sabbath two young men came
down in a boat to visit me, and seeing me look so
poorly, they persuaded me that a sail would do me
good, as I had had a slow fever preying on me for
several days. I thought that it might do me good,

and, placing it among the works of mercy, I consented; but we had no sooner started than I felt convinced of the sin, and insisted on returning. Thus was my conscience again wounded, and I was compelled to keep company with my young irreligious friends. I had no liberty to speak to them on religious subjects, knowing that they might well say, 'Physician, heal thyself!' or, 'First pull out the beam from thine own eye!' I remember that it was with difficulty I could keep my eyes down, I was so constantly moved to raise them to heaven. During the following night I was in a raging fever; and next day, when it intermitted or remitted, I remained in a state of stupidity, or, if roused, in apathy. I envied an old black man, who slept in a garret over my head, and seemed very happy in singing hymns. Annie Stevenson came down, and, finding me so ill, insisted on sending for the doctor. My mother, also, who had been at Belleville, came down to me. My beloved friend, too, walked down (nine miles) to see me the same day, not knowing that my mother had returned. The same exercises of mind continued; but when Mr. Bethune spoke of the vanity of the world at such a time, I told him 'not to speak of the world, for I had done with it forever.' I think that it was the second or third evening after my mother came back that I was, as usual, wondering at the goodness of God in permitting sinners to remain on earth—my mother reading hymns, though I do not know that I was attending to her—when all at once I felt a power of great darkness fall upon me. I felt as if I were hanging over hell by a single hair. Satan seemed to say or suggest, 'You wonder that they and you are out of hell—how can you dwell with everlasting burnings?' Still I felt that this was not a reality, but a temptation. The cold sweat broke out on my face, and my agony was so great that my mother said, 'Joanna, my dear, what is the matter?' 'Oh, mother,' I replied, 'I feel as if I were hanging over the pit! Satan is tempting me!' or words to that effect. She immediately laid down the hymn-book, and, taking up God's own word, began to read of Paul's temptation. God himself, by His Spirit, was dealing with me. Not many minutes after the scene changed, and my mind seemed transported to Mount Calvary, and with the eye of my soul I saw my Savior nailed on the cross, and heard the words, 'It is finished!' There were no thieves, no soldiers, no followers—only the dear Savior himself, hanging on the cross, placed on the summit of a bare mount, His head reclining on His bosom after having uttered these last words of His. I cried out, 'Mother, I see the Savior!' and described the scene. She thought that I was delirious, and said something to compose me to sleep. I replied that it was not with my bodily eyes, but with my mind. . . . I was next transported to the Garden of Gethsemane, and there as plainly I was witness to my blessed Savior's agony, and felt as if He had said, 'All this I endured for thee! This bitter cup I drank to the dregs before I suffered on the cross, and said,

It is finished!' Immediately the fullness and suffi-
ciency of Christ's atonement blazed on my mind. I
saw it a finished work—all the work of Christ, to
which nothing of man's could be added to gain the
favor of God. The burden which had so long pressed
on my shoulders rolled off at the feet of my Jesus,
and looking to the dear Lamb of God, which taketh
away the sin of the world, I cast my good deeds and
my sinful burden on the same spot, and beholding
Him as *my* SAVIOR, I could at last hail Him as '*my*
Lord and *my* God!' I broke out in the fortieth
psalm (Scotch version):

> " 'I waited for the Lord my God,
>   And patiently did bear;
> At length to me He did incline,
>   My voice and cry to hear.
> He took me from the fearful pit,
>   And from the miry clay,
> And on a rock He set my feet,
>   Establishing my way.'

"From that moment all was rapture. The promises I had so long pleaded seemed yea and amen in
Christ Jesus. My mourning was indeed turned into
joy; and Scriptures, hymns, and psalms, and all I
had ever learned, seemed now as clear as a sunbeam;
and from wondering why we were permitted to be
out of hell, I turned to wonder at the glorious plan
of salvation, which God had provided, and why I and
others could not see its fitness, and accept what was
so freely offered without money and without price.
Every thing seemed to be changed; even the face of

Nature—the trees and the fields were clothed with a brighter verdure. I looked up to the sky and exclaimed with the Psalmist (Psalm viii.), 'When I consider the heavens,' etc., etc. I saw emblems of my Savior every where. I looked at the ocean, and thought of His boundless love; at the rocks, and remembered 'the Rock of ages cleft for me;' at the sands on the shore, and considered His tender mercies as countless; in short, I was as full of happiness as I had been of misery; as full of confidence as I had been of doubts; as assured of my interest in Christ, and that my sins had been laid on Him, and that He was the scape-goat, and had fled away with them. The burden of my sins was upon Him, and the robe of His righteousness thrown around me. I wrapped myself in it; and, from that day, I have gone on my way rejoicing. I have often been cold and dead; I have even at times turned aside, as it were, to drink of the waters of Sihon and rivers of Damascus; but He has as often broken the cisterns I had hewed out for myself, and turned me, by His chastising rod, back to the fountain of living waters.

"The communion season being at hand, I insisted on returning to town to be present at it. 'Now,' thought I, 'I can sit down under His shadow with great delight, and His banner over me will be love,' 'because his anger is turned away, and he comforteth me.' My mother and friend not being aware of my extreme weakness, brought me up in a carriage, and I had a dreadful time of it. By the time I reached home I had relapsed; and my fever, which had been bilious remittent, turned to a nervous fever, which confined me to my bed for many weeks. I was often delirious, and even in dreadful spasms. Still I was happy, and thought that I was going to my Savior, but my mother held me down, and would not let me go. It was long before I recovered, if I ever fairly did; and certainly I had not when I was united to my beloved partner the July following. Now we could take sweet counsel together; and I, in my turn, became a help-meet to him—could understand something of the principle of living by faith; and when the dear saint was tried by Providence, and almost ready to give up, I was made the instrument of comforting him, and of pointing to Him in whom are all things for life and godliness. We sought 'the kingdom of God and His righteousness;' and all things necessary, and many more, have been added unto us. When we were completely emptied of ourselves, He filled us with Himself. We had all things in Christ, and Christ in all things."

The foregoing narrative has been given verbatim from Mrs. Bethune's manuscript, as it affords not only an authentic account of her personal experience, but also as it affords to the reader a most pleasing exhibition of the temper and principles which ruled her life throughout. It is much to be regretted that she did not continue her autobiographical record; but she evidently meant to carry it no farther than to her establishment in the Christian faith, and the pe-

D

riod when her history became so blended with that of her Christian husband. Should any one suspect, from some passages in the paper, that she was apt to be carried out of the sound judgment of a sober faith by an excited imagination, it is proper to reply that unreal fancies were very far from being characteristic of her mind, which, with all its energy and spirituality, was unusually chastened and scriptural, founding all its convictions on the testimony of God in Scripture, confirmed by the witness of the Holy Ghost with her spirit. It is not difficult for an observer of the phases which the mind sometimes assumes from sympathy with the body, to see that her thoughts were affected by the brain, heated by fever, and swimming midst the undulations of the disease which had shaken her strength; but the fidelity she observed in writing her recollections savor little of an unwarranted enthusiasm, but rather gives us a beautiful exhibition of a living faith shining through and turning to a heavenly glory the infirmities of the flesh.

CHAPTER VIII.

PLANS OF USEFULNESS.

Mrs. Graham's Correspondence.—Origin of the Monthly Missionary Prayer-meeting. — The Mission to the Indians. — Relief of Poor Widows with Small Children.—New York Orphan Asylum.

It is now proper that we should go back a little in date, to resume the thread of our own continuous narrative.

Mrs. Graham, notwithstanding the incipient and onerous duties of her school, maintained a constant correspondence with pious friends, her former Edinburgh associates in religion and charity, especially with her dear and most intimate, and, as appears from her letters, her strongest-minded friend, Mrs. Baillie Walker. The interchange of pious sentiments between these devoted and intellectual women was highly valued by them both, and, on Mrs. Graham's part, was accepted as the means of increasing her activity and usefulness. In fact, Mrs. Graham endeavored to transfer to New York the same spirit and method of religious activity which she had cultivated in her native land and with her pious Edinburgh friend, and hence the origination of not a few charities, eleemosynary and religious, whose happy influences are felt to this day. It was about this time that, by the reviving blessing of the Holy Ghost, a missionary spirit began to prevail in the evangelical

churches of Great Britain, which, of course, excited
the ardent sympathy of Mrs. Walker and Mrs. Graham. Mrs. Walker lost no time in sending to New
York sermons, reports, and other tracts on these ani-
mating subjects, which Mrs. Graham eagerly received,
and, not willing to confine the pleasure to herself, was
accustomed to call together her most intimate Christian friends for the purpose of reading to them, and
uniting with them in conversation and prayer in reference to the conversion of the world. These private meetings grew in interest and in numbers. Dr.
Rodgers, of the Presbyterian Church, Dr. Mason, of
the Scotch Associate Church, Dr. Livingston, of the
Dutch Church, and some of the Baptist ministers,
whose names have not reached us, were drawn into
their sphere, and it resulted in the establishment (February, 1798) of a monthly missionary prayer-meeting,
held on the evening of the first Wednesday of each
month, in one another's houses of worship, by a union
of the three denominations just named.

Was not this the first monthly concert of prayer
for blessing on the missionary enterprise of modern
times? The first meeting of this kind was held, if I
mistake not, in the Scotch Associate Presbyterian
Church in Cedar Street, then Dr. John M. Mason's;
the second in the Wall Street Presbyterian Church,
then Dr. Rodgers's; another in the Middle Dutch
Church, Nassau Street.* I can not trace them farther.

* See Letters of Mrs. Isabella Graham, No. xiii., to Mrs. W. Bail-

As a natural result of these prayers, a society was founded in New York for sending missionaries among the Indians, and also among the poor scattered settlers on the frontiers. The first annual sermon of this society was preached by the Rev. Dr. Livingston. It is carefully to be noted that a copy of this missionary sermon by Dr. Livingston was one of the publications on the subject which were read by the young pioneers of missions, who prayed under the shelter of the hay-stack at Williamstown. It is pleasing and most instructive thus to trace the links in God's providence toward the accomplishment of His own designs by His blessing on the prayers and zeal of His people.

Mrs. Graham's religion was patterned too closely after the example of her Divine Lord to allow neglect of bodily wants while seeking the salvation of the soul; and so we find that, in the midst of her missionary zeal, which led to the formation of the earliest missionary society, she projected, and carried into successful operation (November, 1797), the "Society for the Relief of Poor Widows with Small Children"—a society which is still flourishing in active usefulness, having been continued, with unremitting energy, by successive almoners of most Christian charity, who have remembered the apostolical injunction, to visit the widows and fatherless in their affliction. I copy from the Memoirs of Mrs. Graham an account of the institution of this society, as it includes the first ef-

lie Walker; also, Mrs. Graham's Life (Tract Society's edition), p. 129, 130, 131.

fort of Mrs. Bethune in the exercise of active benevolence.

"Mr. Bethune, in the year 1796, was one of the distributing managers of the St. Andrew's Society of New York. The relief of this national society being confined to Scotch people, Mrs. Bethune's feelings were much interested for such applicants as could not be helped by her husband's almonership, and she, at the first, collected small sums for their relief; but, anxious to put the charity on a firmer basis, she consulted with some other ladies, called a meeting at Mrs. Graham's house, organized a society under the above title, elected a Board of Managers, and Mrs. Graham First Directress, Mrs. Sarah Hoffman Second Directress, and Mrs. Bethune Third Directress. Many, very many widowed have been made to sing for joy through the timely comfort afforded by the society so established during every year since. Mrs. Graham continued in the chief direction of the Widows' Society for a number of years, and was constantly assisted in the work by her daughter, Mrs. Bethune, until the year 1806.

"It had long before that time been discovered by the ladies of the Widows' Society that some systematic provision should be made for the orphan children of the deceased widows, as it was not within the scope of their society to assist them after the mothers had been taken away. This led, ultimately, to the foundation of the New York ORPHAN ASYLUM, under the care of a society of ladies bearing that name, an account of which will be given hereafter."

CHAPTER IX.

MRS. BETHUNE'S ASSOCIATES.

Sketches of Mrs. Lindsay, Mrs. Chrystie, and Mrs. Mackanness.

FROM what has been said it will be seen that Mrs. Bethune, at the beginning of her open Christian life, enjoyed great advantages of Christian society. Besides the eminent men of the ministry whom we have named, and who were frequent visitors at her mother's house, and the religious spirit in her own family, tradition, rather than record, has preserved the memory of several pious ladies, whom Mrs. Bethune loved for their heartfelt piety, and venerated as examples for their strong intelligence and edifying discretion.

Among these was Mrs. Lindsay, a Scotch lady, wife of Mr. Robert Lindsay, an active member, if not elder, of the Scotch Presbyterian Church. Mr. and Mrs. Lindsay were plain, pious, unpretentious people, who manifested in all their lives the Spirit of their Divine Lord by love of the truth, kindness to the poor, and zeal in every method of advancing the cause of Christ. The author has not been able, though after much search, to find, at this late day, any memorials of Mrs. Lindsay which would display her character; but he would be ungrateful to the memory of one of his mother's most valued friends, and one whom she visited and cherished to the last as a mother in Israel, and a wise, sympathizing counselor for things of time and eternity, did he not preserve on this memorial page the name, now almost forgotten, but one well known and beloved by Christians of New York, of Mrs. Sarah Lindsay. She lived to a very advanced age, closing her pilgrimage in the year 1847, Mrs. Bethune having had the privilege of ministering at her death bedside.

Another of the most intimate and highly-prized friends of Mrs. Graham and her family was Mrs. Chrystie, the widow of Major James Chrystie, of the Revolutionary army. He was by birth a Scotchman; and, having emigrated to Pennsylvania in 1775, ardently adopted the colonial cause, and entered the army as a lieutenant in 1776, from which rank, the year following, he was advanced to a captaincy, being, at the age of twenty-seven, the oldest captain in the Pennsylvania line. Major Chrystie enjoyed, in a special degree, the confidence of General Washington, a striking proof of which was given at the time of the discovery of Arnold's treason. Washington, being anxious to know the state of the garrison at West Point and the neighboring posts, sent (then) Captain Chrystie with verbal orders, not being willing to run the risk of written papers falling into the hands of the enemy. "Has your excellency any farther orders?" asked Captain Chrystie. "Yes," replied the general; "one, and that a very serious one: Captain Chrystie, on this occasion you are not to let me hear of your being taken prisoner. Do you understand me?" "Perfectly well," was the answer; "you shall not hear of that event." Captain Chrystie accomplished his mission in so short a time that Washington, on seeing him approach, supposed that he had been driven back, but was soon reassured and satisfied by the captain's report.

Mrs. Mary Chrystie was the daughter of a Lutheran clergyman, the Rev. John Albert Weygand, a man noted for piety, and learning, and great beauty of person. After finishing his University course at Halle, he lingered for a while in that city, until a heart-sore trial rendered him glad to emigrate (1746) to this country as the minister of a colony from the Palatinate; and in 1748, by the advice and recommendation of the first Lutheran Synod in America, he became the minister of their Church at Reading. Some ten years afterward, Rev. Dr. Muhlenberg writes to his friends in Germany that "he found the Pastor Weygand laboring, with the blessing of God, in New York and its vicinity; and that the congregations under his care were enjoying spiritual peace and prosperity." Mary (Mrs. Chrystie) was about ten years old when her parents moved to New York, where they resided until their deaths. Being left the eldest of the orphan family, the care of her brothers and sisters devolved upon her when a little more than twenty years of age; and she displayed great energy, faithfulness, and prudence in the execution of her trusts, the favor of her God and her father's

God resting upon her exertions. She was married to Major Chrystie in 1781, with whom she lived most happily until March, 1798, when he departed this life, in full reliance on "the finished work of the Redeemer, clinging closely to the cross, at whose foot none ever perished." Mrs. Chrystie was then required to exert herself personally for the care of her family, from which she was soon relieved by her eldest son, thus being permitted to enjoy with greater freedom the pious and intelligent society of the friends she loved, by whom, in turn, she was greatly esteemed and cherished until her death of immortal gain.

Mrs. Chrystie enjoyed an intimate, confidential, and pious friendship with a Mrs. Mackanness, who also became intimate with the circle in which Mrs. Graham and her daughters had the privilege to find delightful intercourse. Of Mrs. Mackanness, the writer of this biography knew little more than that she also was, like Mrs. Chrystie, the wife of a Scotchman; and that, with her friends Mrs. Chrystie and Mrs. Graham, she belonged to the Scotch Church in Cedar Street, at first under the pastoral care of the elder Rev. Dr. John Mason, afterward under that of his yet more distinguished son, the Rev. Dr. John M. Mason. This church association, as it may have been the occasion of the intimacy of these pious women, contributed to perpetuate it while they remained on earth. The name of Mrs. Mackanness was often on the lips of Mrs. Bethune as of a friend greatly beloved, and of a saint whose faith she loved to follow, who inherited the promises.

Mrs. Chrystie was a woman of great loveliness in mind and in person, retaining until the last most charming traces of the rare beauty which distinguished her family. The biographer can not close this brief notice of his mother's friend better than in the words of the Rev. Dr. Hugh Smith, (at one time) of St. Peter's, Chelsea, New York, who has recorded his recollections thus:

. . . "A similar impression was produced on my mind by *one* whose name is associated with all that is active in benevolence or saintly in piety (Mrs. ISA-BELLA GRAHAM). And there was another, the friend of her heart, with whom she often 'took sweet counsel,' who shunned the eye and applause of men while she lived, and whose name, therefore, may not appear upon this humble page [Mrs. Mary Chrystie], but on whom the writer never looked without being reminded of Him who was 'meek and lowly in heart.' It is said that the strength of earthly affection, and the habit of sweet, familiar intercourse, will sometimes cause a change gradually to pass over the features, and assimilate in countenance those who are assimilated in taste and character. Certainly the love and practice of piety—the daily exercise of benevolent feelings and Christian affections, do add a peculiar grace and benignity to the aspect. It was so with *her*. She was lovely amid the wanings of age. A heavenly expression played over her placid and

speaking features; while her soft, musical voice, with
its silvery tones, seemed already attuned to accompany the golden harps of heaven in the 'song of the
redeemed.' Years have elapsed since she departed
'to be with Christ;' but her countenance, with its radiant expression, is distinctly before me, and my ears
seem to drink in again the mellow sounds they loved
to hear. These were saints indeed. 'Their witness
was on high; their record was above.' They were
not of our external communion; but truly their 'fel-
lowship was with the Father, and His Son, Jesus
Christ;' and deeply had they drunken of His Spirit.
'They rest from their labors, and their works do follow them.'"

Mrs. Chrystie was survived by her son, Albert
Chrystie, Esq., who married Frances, daughter of the
very distinguished *Colonel William Fen* (one of the
framers of the American Constitution, member of the
first Senate of the United States, etc., etc., etc.), orig-
inally of Georgia, but, after his marriage with Catharine, daughter of Commodore James Nicholson, a resident of New York, who died August 7th, 1854, on
her ninetieth birthday. Mr. Chrystie inherited, with
a strong personal resemblance to his mother, her pious, retiring, benevolent, and zealous character. Mr.
Chrystie, at the time of his death, was a greatly beloved elder of the Reformed Dutch Church of Has-
tings, upon the Hudson, a church he helped to found,
and whose continued prosperity is a monument to his
worth. "Having the refinement and polish of the

circle in which he had always moved, with a heart of unaffected kindness, the only and unfailing source of true courtesy, he evinced, wherever he went, the bearing of a thorough Christian gentleman, and commanded universal respect." Mr. Chrystie died in 1856, in his 67th year.

Mrs. Mackanness, another intimate associate of this period, whose name was often on Mrs. Bethune's lips, and never without expressions of affectionate reverence, was the early and intimate friend of Mrs. Chrystie, being mentioned in her journal as the instrument of her brother-in-law's conversion. She was a woman of strong mind, warm feelings, and most elevated piety. With dignity of manner that almost inspired awe, and ever checked frivolity and levity, she yet inspired confidence and love. Her imagination was not lively, but common sense marked all her acts. So clear and discriminating was her mind, and so pure her conduct, that the ascendency she possessed over all who approached her was almost unbounded —ever mingled with the deepest reverence. The storms of the Revolutionary War swept over the youthful days of Mrs. Mackanness and Mrs. Chrystie. The stirring scenes of that period, so full of toil, care, and perplexity to American women, cemented their young hearts; and the blasting of early hopes taught them to look beyond the blessings of this world, and to cast the anchor of their souls above, where "no sad changes come." . . . They walked meekly and quietly here, and both departed peacefully to take possession of mansions on high; not there to lose the kindly affections of love and joy which had refreshed them in their path through the wilderness, but, having laid down the clogs of earth, they are forever "filled with all the fullness of God."

It is said of Mrs. Mackanness that her joy and confidence, when dying, exhibited a perfect victory over the last enemy. "All," said she, at one time, "all that we have ever seen, all that we have ever heard, are bubbles—bubbles now!" Even when her mind wandered, the same heavenly peace possessed her soul; and, imagining that she saw her departed friends, she joyfully saluted them by name, bowing her head and smiling in the most animated and delighted manner. Mrs. Mackanness died in New York, after a very short illness, on the 17th day of March, 1806.

The intimacy between the Mackanness and the Bethune family must have been close; and it would seem, from the following obituary notice written by Mr. Bethune, that there were business as well as social relations between them.

"Sacred to the memory of *Thomas Thornton Mackanness*, co-partner in the house of Divie Bethune & Co., and son to Thomas Mackanness, Esq.: a most excellent youth, endeared to his parents and relatives by all that is tender and dutiful, and to society by all that is amiable and upright. He fell a victim to the yellow fever, on the 10th of September, 1805, aged 22 years.

"The bliss in God's rich promise given,
   This child of faith and prayer
Found not on earth, so fled to heaven,
   To taste its fullness there.
     *   *   *   *   *   *
Nor youth, nor wealth, nor love could save
   His body from the tomb;
But Jesus triumphed o'er the grave,
   And took his spirit home."

CHAPTER X.

INTRODUCTION OF SUNDAY-SCHOOLS.

Journey to Scotland.—Sunday-school Movement there.—Mr. and
Mrs. Bethune's Labors in New York in 1802.—The Mother of
Sabbath-schools in America.—Plans of Usefulness.

For a number of these years the health of Mrs.
Bethune suffered greatly from several causes, which
shattered her nervous system to a degree from which
she did not recover until late in life. There is, con-
sequently, little to record of active engagements during this period. In 1801, Mr. Bethune, hoping to get
benefit for the invalid, took his wife and eldest child,
Jessy, to Great Britain, that they might visit the place
of his birth (Dingwall, Ross-shire, Scotland) and their
surviving friends. They returned to New York in
September, 1802. Their visit to Scotland was, in one
particular, attended by a remarkable result.

"As early as 1797 a public movement was made
in Edinburgh in favor of Sunday-schools in Scotland.
A number of pious persons of various denominations
had, for a few months, been in the habit of meeting
to pray for the advancement of religion at home and
abroad. The duty of accompanying their prayers
with personal exertions naturally occurred to them,
and led their minds to the education of poor children. They formed 'The Edinburgh Gratis Sab-

bath-school Society,' to raise and conduct Sabbath evening schools in Edinburgh and its vicinity, in which schools the Christian doctrines common to the associated denominations only were to be taught, and the duties all to be performed, without pay, by the members of the society. This procedure became rapidly popular, and was imitated by other cities, and soon throughout Scotland." The circle in Edinburgh with whom this good work began was one to which Mr. and Mrs. Bethune would most likely be introduced, and a scheme so consonant to their dispositions must have arrested their attention. Hence we are not surprised to learn that, "in New York, the late Mr. Bethune, assisted by his lady and her mother, had, at their own expense, opened a school as early as 1802 [the year after their return from Scotland], and, shortly after, several more, in other parts of the city, and personally superintended them."*

The author deeply regrets that his searches have failed to discover any authentic records of these schools; but, from various consenting circumstances, is strongly inclined to believe that the Edinburgh movement had its origin farther back than the public society, the date of which is given by Mr. Green (1797), and that it arose in that pious circle of which Mrs. Baillie Walker, and, until her death, Lady Glenorchy, with other devoted Christians, were active

---

* See speech of Timothy R. Green, Esq., at the New York Sunday-school JUBILEE, in *Sunday Journal* of that date.

members, and to which Mrs. Graham, during her residence in Edinburgh, belonged. The correspondence
closely maintained between Mrs. Baillie Walker and
Mrs. Graham was, as we have seen, the medium by
which the reviving missionary spirit was transmitted
from Scotland to this country; and we also know
that Mrs. Graham was engaged personally in teaching a school for young women on Sabbath evenings
as early as 1792–3. The synchronism was not acci-
dental. However, be that as it may, we can not doubt
that Mrs. Bethune's mind received its strong impulse
toward Sabbath-schools during her visit to Scotland
in 1801–2. The impulse was never lost; but ill
health, the birth and care of children, and occupation
in other enterprises (particularly the formation and
establishment of the New York Orphan Asylum,
1806, etc.), prevented it from so fully occupying
her mind until many years afterward, 1814, when increasing attention to Sunday-schools in England, ac-
counts of which were communicated to Mr. and Mrs.
Bethune by the godly Stephen Bush, of Bristol, England, roused Mr. and Mrs. Bethune to similar efforts.
The Sabbath-schools of Scotland were combined in a
National Union in 1816; the Female Sabbath-school
Union of New York was formed through the efforts
of Mrs. Bethune in the same year, though the immediate influence which operated in this latter case
came rather from England, though the formation of
the Sabbath Union by Mrs. Bethune was the ripe
growth of seed sown and cultivated from the year
1802.

It would be inconsistent with the meek spirit of her whose life we are writing to claim for her the honors of a doubtful precedence; and certainly no one rejoiced more than she did in the several efforts to establish Sunday-schools in different parts of the country; but the facts and dates thus given show that Providence intended for Mrs. Bethune the distinction of being the mother of Sabbath-schools in America.

It should also be noted that, about this period, Mrs. Graham became anxious for the instruction of the children of the widows, pensioners of the Widows' Society, and, consulting with her daughter, devised a plan for teaching them, and others similarly situated, by the voluntary agency of young ladies; and, "on the 17th of February, 1804," Mrs. Graham writes (Life, p. 231), "twenty-nine young ladies met, with Mrs. (Sarah) Hoffman and myself, at Mr. O(gden) Hoffman's, Wall Street; and, having separated themselves in pairs, devoted themselves" to a work not a little resembling the Industrial and similar schools of the present day, except that all the teaching was supplied gratuitously. There were, at this time, no public schools, free-schools, or Sabbath-schools; and it is easy to see how, from the experience she must have had in those week-day schools, Mrs. Bethune's conviction of the usefulness of schools on the Sabbath was greatly strengthened, although her home-cares as a young mother, increased by her delicate health, did not permit her to engage as entirely as her inclination would otherwise have led her to do.

Mrs. Graham, since the removal of Mr. and Mrs. Andrew Smith (her third daughter) to Virginia in 1803, had consented to reside permanently with Mr. and Mrs. Bethune. This brought the three benevolent spirits into constant and close communion, the results of which pious alliance have been seen in several important enterprises. Mrs. Graham's personal individual exertions for religion and charity are related in her Life, prepared by Mr. and Mrs. Bethune conjointly, and published after her death, a more full and carefully corrected edition of which was arranged, with the addition of much matter not in the first edition, the copyright of which was presented to the American Tract Society, and it was published by them with her full and entire approval and authentication.

CHAPTER XI.

THE ORPHAN ASYLUM.

Mrs. Bethune's Plans. — Life of Francke. — Mrs. Hoffman.—Mr. Bethune's Address. — Public Meeting. — Society formed. — The Fundamental Principle.—Power of Faith. — The first Home.— Larger Accommodations.—The Asylum at Bloomingdale.—Mrs. Bethune's Agency, Service, and Resignation. — Action of the Board of Managers.

THE story of Mr. and Mrs. Bethune's large and intelligent philanthropy can not here be told; but, as each was individually active, their union rendered their usefulness vastly more than trebly efficient under the Divine blessing. Their evenings were spent in constructing and maturing plans for doing good; all the leisure of their days in executing them. The three discussed among themselves the question how the children of the deceased widows should be provided for, as the Widows' Society were not to be allowed to do any thing for them, though many were left without any means of support.

About this time a copy of a Life of Francke, with a history of his Orphan House at Halle, fell into the hands of Mrs. Bethune. It became a study for the three around their fireside, and was regarded as a means used by Providence to assist them in their benevolent difficulty. "I will remain with the widows," said Mrs. Graham; "but you, my dear Joanna, are younger; do you leave the active direction of the Widows' Society, and devote yourself to your heavenly Father's children, the fatherless and the motherless." After careful and not hasty deliberation, their pious friends were called into council, especially Mrs. SARAH HOFFMAN, whose excellent judgment, strengthened by much experience in charity, and commanding social position, rendered it peculiarly desirable that the movement should be made under her auspices; and it was determined that an appeal should be made to the benevolent public of New York for the means and agencies necessary to the founding of an Orphan Asylum, which should receive under its protecting roof all legitimate children left orphans by the death of both parents. Mr. Bethune was requested to write a call for a public meeting of ladies for the purpose of organizing such an institution, which was published in the spring of 1806.

"The helpless condition of orphan children has often awakened the compassion of every feeling heart. The exertions of the Ladies' Society [for the Relief of Widows with Small Children] provided, in a great measure, for the children of widows; but there exists, at present, no society whose peculiar province it is to rescue from want, from danger, and from misery the ORPHAN CHILD. It is therefore proposed to establish a female society to provide an asylum for orphan children; and, as the funds of such an institution must come from the generosity of a benevolent public, annual subscriptions are respectfully solicited from both ladies and gentlemen. As soon as a sufficient number of female subscribers are procured, a general meeting will be called to form a Constitution and make other requisite arrangements.

> " 'The friendless babe, whom want alarms,
> Cast on life's desert wild,
> To you extends its feeble arms—
> Oh, save the orphan child.' "

Accordingly, on the 15th of March, 1806, a public meeting was held at the City Hotel (then occupying the block on the west side of Broadway, between Thames and Cedar Streets), and the New York Orphan Asylum Society was organized, Mrs. Sarah Hoffman being chosen First Directress, Mrs. General HAMILTON Second Directress, Mrs. Bethune Treasurer (Mrs. SARAH STARTIN some years afterward succeeding her, Mrs. Bethune's health at the time not being very strong), with ten other influential ladies, members of the Board of Managers.

At the very outset of their operations the Board adopted as a principle of their management that, relying upon God's own promise to be "the Father of the fatherless," they would never refuse an orphan child brought to them for protection, whether they had a dollar in the treasury or not. From this rule the Society, up to this hour, has never swerved, nor is it likely, after their rich experience of the Divine care, that they ever will. It was always Mrs. Bethune's opinion, as often expressed in her conversa-

tion respecting the conduct of charities, that any
"skimping" (a Scotch term, having no synonym in
English), especially in limiting the number of the
truly necessitous objects, was a species of distrust in
God; and the hoarding or putting away at interest
money for which Providence asked a present use
was an unbelief more likely to bring loss than secure
future advantage. In several cases, during the early years of the Asylum, children were brought to its
door when the funds were utterly expended; but
they were gladly welcomed, and soon means came in
to supply their wants. So, in cases of much larger
expenditure, the only question in the mind of Mrs.
Bethune and her associates would be, "Is the expenditure actually necessary for the welfare and comfort of the orphans?" This being decided in the affirmative, the expense was at once increased. Nor
did the Lord ever fail to answer the trust of his handmaiden. I have often heard my mother say that, in
any time of need, a few words stating that the funds
of the Society needed replenishing, thrown into a
newspaper, was sure to bring in donations equal to
the need; more frequently, the money came in before the appeal was made.

The ladies began their asylum in a hired two-sto-
ried frame house in the village of Greenwich (then
the upper part of New York City), where a few children were carefully sheltered and instructed, under
the watch of a competent matron. It soon became
manifest that much larger accommodations should be

provided for their proposed charges; and the ladies, in the courage of their faith, were ready to follow God's leadings in the emergency. They had begun to accumulate a fund for building, but it did not exceed $350. Notwithstanding, true to their governing principle, they at once resolved to erect a suitable house. They contracted for a site of liberal size, nearly an acre of ground, in Bank Street, not far from Mr. Bethune's place, giving ample space for playground, garden, and fresh air, on which they put up a handsome, though plain structure, fifty feet square, all at a cost of about $25,000. Mrs. Bethune and Mrs. Startin managed the finances with great skill and liberality—Mrs. Startin freely making advances, when needed, from her own handsome means, and Mrs. Bethune obtaining a pledge of her husband's credit for thousands of dollars rather than the building should be delayed. The debt that remained at its completion was soon swept off by donations and legacies; besides which, the growth of the city gave much increased value to the property, that the original asylum was, in 1840, replaced by a noble building of most extensive accommodation on the banks of the Hudson, at Bloomingdale, surrounded by ten acres of ground, and the Society enriched by a large funded property from the accumulation of legacies. The Orphan Asylum Society was never so useful or so liberally sustained as it is now (1861), and there can be but little doubt of its continuing to be a monument of pious enterprise, and a fountain of charita-

ble goodness, while the great city which has so liberally supported it sits like a queen on the waves.

The honor of originating the Orphan Asylum has
been popularly given to Mrs. Graham; but the facts
were as we have stated them, and it belongs, at least,
equally to her daughter. They were both at the beginning of it; and, although Mrs. Graham continued
in the direction of the Widows' Society, she was,
through her daughter, almost equally interested for
the orphans as her daughter continued to be for the
widows. It was a partnership in benevolence toward the two special objects of Christian charity,
"the widows and orphans in their affliction." Indeed, Mrs. Graham consented to be elected a trustee
of the Orphan Asylum in the spring of 1810, finding association with her daughter in the Orphan Society more easy for her advanced age than service,
separated from her, in that of the Widows' Society.

Mrs. Bethune continued to serve as Trustee or
Treasurer in the Orphan Asylum until the death of
her dear friend and long-loved associate, Mrs. Hoffman, when, Mrs. General Hamilton being elected First
Directress, Mrs. Bethune was chosen to succeed Mrs.
Hamilton as Second; and, on Mrs. Hamilton's resignation of the First Directress-ship, Mrs. Bethune succeeded her venerable friend as the presiding officer,
which place she continued to hold until May, 1859.
Long before this, however, Mrs. Bethune, conscious
of increasing infirmities, had wished the ladies, her
associates, to relieve her of her office. Thus we find

on the minutes of the Board, April, 1851, the following letter from Mrs. Bethune, with the expression of the Board concerning it:

Mrs. Bethune's First Letter of Resignation, April, 1851.

"DEAR LADIES,—We read, Psalm xc., 10, 'The days of our years are threescore years and ten; and if, by reason of strength, they be fourscore years, yet is their strength labor and sorrow, for it is soon cut off, and we fly away.' These words of the Psalmist have been constantly in my mind for some time past, but particularly since the fall which I had last summer, which so enfeebled my health that my own family and my duties in the Orphan Asylum were necessarily neglected. Another portion of Scripture God impressed on my mind last winter: 'Set thy house in order, for thou shalt die and not live.' The above, with some circumstances which I forbear to mention, have convinced me that it is my duty to resign my place as First Directress of the Orphan Asylum Society, a place I have held but a few years, and in which I may not have been so efficient as my predecessor (Mrs. Hamilton). I therefore beg, my dear ladies, that you will accept my resignation, and appoint one younger in years, and who can have more aid than I have. I shall not cease to pray for your prosperity; but, like the children of Israel banished from their beloved Jerusalem, will say of the Orphan Asylum, 'If I forget THEE, let my right hand forget her cunning!' But, dear ladies, while I resign my place as Directress, I still claim the privilege of visiting and acting on the School Committee.

"The Orphan Asylum was the last place my beloved mother visited, and gave to the inmates religious instruction. A few days after she ceased from her labors and entered her rest, thirty-seven years ago. Her last words to me were, 'My dear, you and I have long been engaged in charitable labors, and have experienced how little can be done in reforming the old, and therefore I beg that you will devote yourself to the young.'

"Kneeling at her coffin, I prayed my Savior to permit me to give instruction to the dear lambs of our orphan fold. Great has been HER reward; for many, I trust, have joined her in heaven. One of our first orphans visited me a few years ago, and told me that the earliest time he could remember was standing at Mrs. Graham's knee, and repeating texts of Scripture after her, for he was too young to read. That child still lives, a highly respected minister of the Gospel in this state.

"My ever-to-be-lamented husband also took a deep interest in the institution, and gave religious instruction to its inmates, chiefly on the Sabbath. I rejoice that our highly respected neighbor, Mr. Pelatiah Perit, now so kindly supplies his place. My prayer to God is, that he may long continue his labors of love after I shall have entered into my rest, and the hand that now writes will be mouldering in the grave.

"I remain, dear ladies, respectfully and affectionately, your fellow-laborer,   JOANNA BETHUNE.
  "New York, April, 1851."

The above letter was received by the Board with
great sorrow; and it was "unanimously resolved that
we can not accept the resignation of our venerated
friend, but earnestly request her to continue at the
head of the Board of Direction, and to accept the assurance of our sincere desire to relieve her of care
and fatigue in any way she may permit."*

Subsequently we find another note addressed by
her to the Board, the date of which is wanting:

"MY DEAR LADIES,—Considering my age and increasing infirmities, I can not expect to be long in
your Board. I have tendered my resignation several times, but I need not inform you that it has never been accepted.

"Next to my own family, the Orphan Asylum
stands first in my affections; indeed, it is never out
of my mind, by day or by night. I bless God that,
when I am called home, I shall leave it in such prosperous circumstances. I need not say that our accommodations are not equal to the wants of our large
family; and that, such being the case, I suggested the
necessity of adding a wing to the building as soon
as our means would permit, and I thought that those
who heard me approved of it. I have also thought
that, some years hence, another wing would be necessary. It may be that some of the Board might

* Minutes of the Board, May 6th, 1851.

think it best to sell the property, and remove farther from the city. This to me, and others, is not desirable. . . . Where can we find a more suitable situation—so near the city, and so easy of access—so near the Hudson, and exhibiting so well our beautiful front to the numerous passengers on the river? . . ."

The Board, at their meeting, May 26th, 1859, thought themselves required, by their duty to the institution, to adopt the following minute:

"Mrs. Bethune being prevented, by her removal to Brooklyn and by the infirmities of advanced age, from engaging any longer in the direction of the Society, and the duties she so much loved and so faithfully performed from its very formation, it was resolved that Mrs. John Anthon be appointed First Directress, and Mrs. Van Horne Second Directress; also, that the name of Mrs. Bethune, while living, be always published above the names of the Board of Direction."

The last time Mrs. Bethune met with the Board was at the anniversary held in the Asylum at Bloomingdale, May 13th, 1856, as shown by the following minute of that date:

"Mrs. Bethune, the venerable First Directress and surviving founder of the institution, was present. The Rev. Dr. Bethune made the address."

This completed fifty years of service rendered by her to the Asylum. She attended the meetings of the Board regularly up to June of the year before. She never knew of her ceasing to be in office.

The following extract from the 55th Annual Report of the Orphan Asylum Society closes the record of my mother's connection with an institution which shared more deeply her love and care than any other. "My dear," said she one day, when playfully reproaching herself for some slip of memory, "I believe that I shall forget every thing but the Orphan Asylum; that I shall always remember."

"Since the last annual report of this society, the last tie has been severed that bound it to its commencement—a link which extended through a chain of years from its very foundation has been broken, gently separated, leaving the Board of Direction, as it were, themselves orphans—in the loss of Mrs. Jo- ANNA BETHUNE, the mother of this institution, the original proposer of its plan.

"Mrs. BETHUNE was, before this society existed, deeply interested in that which takes care of widows with young children; and often, as these poor widows died, and left their fatherless and now motherless little ones, her kind heart grieved that they could no longer receive from that society the aid they needed more than ever. Hence, by a natural step, the foundation of the New York Orphan Asylum, the first call for which was from the pen of Mr. DIVIE BE- THUNE, at the request of his wife and her associates in the Widows' Society. From this period until absolutely disabled by the infirmities of age, a period of little less than fifty years, Mrs. BETHUNE's heart and hand, prayers and active exertions, were ever engaged, successively as Trustee, Treasurer, Second Directress, and First Directress, in behalf of the blessed work she had undertaken. She died on the 28th of July, 1860, at the age of ninety-two years; and when, from the bed of suffering and weariness, she woke in the glory of an immortality inconceivable to mortal mind, we can fancy, amid the ecstatic joy of the first moment of bliss, that one source of delight, and not the least, would be the sight of the many happy, glorified spirits who, but for her instrumentality, might have languished here in want, and died ignorant or neglectful of the glorious inheritance purchased for them by their precious Savior.

"We dare not trust ourselves to lift, in imagination, the veil that separates us from that unseen world; it would make us so envy her, so long to be there, that we could not, without repining, turn back to earth, and its cares and sin. But may such a life as hers, with the reward we know she now enjoys, be a spur to our zeal, and inspire us never to weary nor faint, but work on and rejoice that we may bear a humble part in the great scheme of making the world happier and better."

CHAPTER XII.

MRS. HOFFMAN AND MRS. STARTIN.

The Associates of Mrs. Bethune.—Mrs. Hoffman and Mrs. Startin.
—Their Character and Services.—Testimonies of the Board.

IT is to be lamented that so little has been preserved of the excellent women who were associated
with Mrs. Bethune in the foundation and early progress of the Orphan Asylum. The writer has taken
great pains to discover whatever remains concerning
them on record or in the memory of the people, but
he has not been as successful as he desired and hoped.

Mrs. Sarah Hoffman was the contemporary rather
of Mrs. Graham than of her daughter, but Mrs. Bethune held her in that respect and veneration which
her strong mind, benevolent character, and dignified
carriage were so well calculated to inspire; and that
this regard was not unreciprocated is seen in the fact
that Mrs. Hoffman preferred to resign her directress-
ship of the older society to preside over the Orphan
Asylum Board, which was more especially the enterprise of her younger friend. Unless she had done so,
Mrs. Bethune would not have had the same courage
for the untried work; but Mrs. Hoffman's name was
as a tower of strength, so high was her moral and intellectual position in the best society of New York at

E 2

that time. There is an affectionate tribute to her memory in the Life of Mrs. Graham (p. 167, American Tract Society's edition), written by Mr. and Mrs. Bethune. Mrs. Graham "and her venerable companion, Mrs. Sarah Hoffman, Second Directress of the Widows' Society, traveled many a day, and took many a step together in the walks of charity. Mrs. Graham was a Presbyterian, Mrs. Hoffman an Episcopalian. Those barriers of which such an unhappy use has been made by sectarians to separate children of God fell down between these two friends at the cry of affliction, and were consumed on the altar of Christian love. Arm in arm, and heart to heart, they visited the abodes of distress, dispensing temporal aid from the purse of charity, and spiritual comfort from the Word of God." Mrs. Hoffman continued her active superintendence of the affairs of the society until 1817, after which her age and infirmities forbade her to continue her much-loved employment, and her attendance at the meetings of the Board almost entirely ceased, though it was not until August, 1821, that her spirit returned to God. Mrs. Hoffman recommended to the ladies the election of Mrs. Startin as her successor. Mrs. Startin was accordingly elected, but declined in favor of Mrs. Hamilton, who, every way fitted for the responsible office, was, as the second directress, from the beginning the one to whom, in the judgment of the Board, the honor was due.

Extract from the Minutes of the Board of Trustees of the Orphan Asylum, August 7, 1821:

"It becomes the duty of the Board this day to record the decease of their late beloved and very venerable directress, Mrs. SARAH HOFFMAN. Eminent in the discharge of her relative duties, in humble hope and ardent faith, and in all the walks of usefulness appropriate to the children of God, she was particularly distinguished by her early, persevering, affectionate, and successful exertions in the cause of the orphan, in the establishment of the society and of the asylum which now affords support and protection to so large a number of otherwise friendless children.

"For many years she was associated with another benevolent member of this Board, whose death was formerly recorded, Mrs. Isabella Graham, in the care of the widow and the fatherless; and in later years, with the lamented Secretary of this Board, Miss Isabella W. Ogden, called away in the vigor of youth.

"As they had remembered the commandments of their God in life, so their God remembered their souls at the hour of death, enabling them to triumph over all its terrors, in the blissful hope of eternal life; and that dark valley, from which human nature, destitute of religion, shrinks back with horror, they entered with a cheerful composure, beholding a ray of heavenly light, leading them on to the regions of immortal glory. The smile of Him who was wounded for their sins and bruised for their iniquities, that He might become their Redeemer, evidently shone on their departing spirits. 'The Eternal God was their refuge, and underneath them the everlasting arms.' 'Blessed are the dead who die in the Lord.'"

Mrs. Hoffman was the daughter of Mr. David Ogden, of Newark, N. J.   Her brothers were Nicholas, Abraham, Isaac, Samuel, and Peter Ogden.   She married Mr. Nicholas Hoffman, by whom she had two sons, Josiah Ogden, afterward Judge Hoffman, and Martin Hoffman, with whom she resided after her husband's death, in Broadway, near Amity Street. Mr. Ogden Hoffman's first wife was a Miss Colden, and it was at her house, in Wall Street, that Mrs. Sarah Hoffman and Mrs. Graham met to organize an association of young ladies for teaching schools among the poor, as recorded by Mrs. Graham, 1804.

Mrs. Sarah Startin was one of those on whom, from the beginning of the institution in 1806, the asylum rested.   Elected a member of the first Board of Trustees, she contributed her wisdom, faith, and courage during the difficulties of organizing the charity and bringing it before the Christian community for support.   Mrs. Startin was the widow of an eminent English merchant, so holding a high place in society; and the estimation in which she was held as an intelligent, consistent Christian, enabled her to commend it effectually to the patronage of the best as well as the most influential people in the city, and thus contributed to make broad the foundations of its future great prosperity.   At the first Mrs. Bethune cheerfully undertook the office of Treasurer, but her feeble health, with the cares of her family, compelled her to resign it at the end of two years, when (1809) Mrs. Startin was chosen to succeed her, and continued to serve until 1821. We find the following minute in the records of the Board in April of that year:

" One circumstance is attended with painful interest to the Board—the resignation of their respected Treasurer. Deep are their feelings of gratitude and affection on recurring to the services of their beloved friend. At the origin of the society, when the magnitude of the object seemed almost to appall the firmest mind—when a building was to be erected, and there were no resources—their benevolent coadjutor became personally responsible for large amounts of money, which enabled them to complete a commodious and well-finished house. The prudence and economy she has ever manifested in discharging her office inspired implicit confidence in her judgment and discretion. Many a child of affliction can bear testimony to the maternal kindness with which she gladdened the heart of the orphan. Her counsels will always be cherished as the result of mature and conscientious reflection. The Board earnestly hope that, although she declines the arduous office of treasurer, she will not resign her situation as trustee, but will continue to animate and encourage them by her countenance and advice. In the retirement of domestic life, long may she enjoy the consolations which flow from the reflections of a well-spent life! Long may she be spared to her friends and associates as their example, to render the various talents of wealth, of influence, and of leisure conducive to the end for which they were given!"

The following is found in the Annual Report for 1822:

"Since the last annual meeting the Board have been bereaved of their First Directress (Mrs. Hoff-man) and late Treasurer, Mrs. Startin, to whom they were accustomed to look for counsel and assistance in every season of discouragement and doubt. In reflecting on the characters of their venerable asso-ciates, whose loss we now lament, we admire the bright example they afforded of active benevolence, and a piety steadfast as it was sincere, which warmed while it elevated the heart, and shone with great and greater lustre unto the perfect day. The memory of these ladies is deeply engraven on the hearts of the Board as they recollect the spirit of charity which pervaded their intercourse in life, and their unwea-ried diligence in accomplishing the plan of this Or-phan Asylum, and rejoice to know that on them has descended 'the blessing of many ready to perish.'"

CHAPTER XIII.

MRS. GENERAL HAMILTON.

Mrs. Hamilton and Mrs. Bethune compared.—Their Attachment.—
Mrs. Hamilton's Parentage.—Early Life.—Married Life.—Death
of Alexander Hamilton.—Mrs. Hamilton in Social Life.—In New
York and Washington.—Her declining Years.—Death and Bur-
ial.

BUT the fellow-worker with whom Mrs. Bethune
was the longest and most intimately associated, and
whom she loved best, while she loved all, was Mrs.
General Hamilton. My mother's regard and esteem
for this venerable lady continually increased. Both
were of determined disposition, neither ready to yield
to the other when they differed, as they sometimes
did, about any matter of policy. Mrs. Bethune was
the more cautious, Mrs. Hamilton the more impuls-
ive, so that occasions of earnest dispute did occur;
but it was charming to see how affectionately these
temporary altercations soon terminated in mutual
embraces, and their love deepened into stronger confidences. Inheriting a fond respect for my mother's
beloved and loving friend, I shall indulge myself with
a brief sketch of her life and character.

Elizabeth Schuyler was the second daughter of
General Philip Schuyler and Catharine Van Rensselaer. The character of General Schuyler is historic-

al. The name of Van Rensselaer was distinguished
for courage, kindliness, and modest dignity. They
are among the wealthiest proprietors of the Dutch
population. Stephen Van Rensselaer, a cousin of
Mrs. Hamilton, and married to her sister, was the
good *Patroon*, deriving that title from his being the
owner of a large manor, embracing the northern portion of Albany County and a large portion of Rensselaer. Mrs. Hamilton was born at Albany on the
9th of August, 1757. Her father's house was the re-
sort of the most distinguished persons in what Wal-
pole, about this period, styled "the proud and opulent Colony of New York;" and, at the opening of
the contest with Great Britain, there came leading
men from distant colonies to hold conference with
General Schuyler, whose sagacity, energy, and noble-
ness of spirit made him the depositary of the most
sacred confidences in those councils which gave birth
to an empire. His daughter Elizabeth thus entered
social life with every advantage of position, and, in
the coterie which gathered around the governor's colonial court in the city of New York, was soon distinguished as a belle. Her person was small and
delicately formed; her face agreeable, and, animated
by her brilliant black eyes, showing and radiating
the spirit and intelligence so fully exhibited in her
subsequent life. The commotions beginning in 1775
confined the family of General Schuyler to their spa-
cious mansion in Albany during the winter, and, during the summer, to his beautiful country estate on

the Hudson, at Saratoga (now Schuylerville), near the scene of the battle of Saratoga. The advance of Burgoyne drove the ladies of the family, with the whole female population of the region, flying from the savages which that commander had adopted among his royal forces. General Schuyler was absent with the army when his children were thus obliged to abandon the beautiful and beloved home of their youth; but, in the midst of their sore trial, they manifested their father's blood; for, as the wheatfields of the wide domain were white to the harvest, Mrs. Hamilton's eldest sister Angelica (afterward Mrs. John B. Church, of Angelica, N. Y.), choosing a moment when the wind was high, with her own hand set fire to the ripe grain, that it might not be gathered for the comfort of the enemy. It was only a few weeks after that General Burgoyne, a prisoner with his staff, was received into the mansion of General Schuyler, whose delicate hospitalities he afterward gratefully acknowledged from his place in Parliament. Thus some of the most brilliant British aristocracy were added to the circle of which Elizabeth Schuyler was the charming ornament; but the gayety was short lived, as Albany soon became again a place of seclusion, whose quiet was disturbed only by the thunders of distant war, or the nearer alarms of savage enemies. The third year after this, General Schuyler, called, at the urgent instance of Washington, to aid the vigorous efforts then making for the revival of his reduced and gallant army, repaired

to the head-quarters of his chief, then at Morristown,
N. J., where Mrs. Schuyler and his daughter accompanied him. Alexander, then Colonel Hamilton, and
confidential aid to the great chief, was soon fascinated
by the brilliant graces of the daughter, who, not less
pleased by the fascinating manners of the distinguished young soldier, yielded to his addresses, and they
were soon married, remaining some time in camp,
until circumstances favored her removal to Albany,
while Colonel Hamilton pursued his gallant duties in
the march to Yorktown; and his letters to his young
bride speak beautifully of his affections and his pa-
triotic valor. The surrender of Cornwallis soon followed; and, on the cessation of warlike operations,
Colonel Hamilton repaired to Albany, where his wife
and their new-born child welcomed him to repose.
Here Hamilton pursued the study of law, and was
admitted to practice. About this time, as Continent-
al Receiver, he attended the Legislature of New York
at Poughkeepsie, and drafted the first legislative resolutions that were framed recommending a Convention to provide a national Constitution for the United
States—the embodiment of a thought which his great
mind had conceived and zealously nourished for some
time previously. Soon after, we find him as a representative of New York in Congress, a leading par-
ticipant in the most important preparatory measures
for the establishment of the present government.

After the peace General Hamilton removed with
his family to the city of New York, where he soon

rose to the highest place at the bar, while, as a member of the New York Legislature, and delegate to the Convention which framed the Federal Constitution, as well as to that which adopted it, his civic fame became as great as his military glory.   Thus, when the government was organized, he took the highest position in the country, next to that of Washington, as Secretary of the Treasury.   During these absorbing public engagements, Mrs. Hamilton assumed the cares of their increased family, and presided over the hospitalities of their home, whose attractions rendered it the centre of a circle distinguished by the society of the most eminent persons, native born and from abroad, then residing at the seat of government.   After resigning his place in the cabinet, Hamilton resumed his professional career in New York (1795), where he resided until his melancholy death.   His house was the scene of most refined and generous hospitality, whether in town or at his summer residence on Harlem Heights, which afforded him and Mrs. Hamilton opportunities for cultivating those elegant tastes in rural pleasures which had been the delight of her early youth on the banks of the Hudson, in beautiful Saratoga.

The religious thankfulness with which she enjoyed these bountiful dispensations of Providence called into vigorous life the principles of piety which had directed her education under her father's care, and were preparing her for the deep sorrows of her later life.   The admonition of her dying husband, the victim of a political murder, most lamentable and execrable, "Remember, Eliza, you are a Christian!" showed his confidence in her faith, as well as his own recognition of its Divine source. Deeply did she need its upholding consolations. Her eldest son had already fallen a victim to a similar bloodthirsty violence when her great sorrow came; and a beloved daughter, losing her reason amid the sudden horrors of her father's death, became the sad charge of her bleeding heart.

Mrs. Hamilton bore her calamities with fortitude and resignation, but sought her subsequent enjoyments for this world in the offices of a religious life and a most active charity, which she continued to practice up to the very close of her unusually protracted life, in her ninety-seventh year. She retained both her mental and physical faculties to the last; and when at Washington, during her latest years, for the prosecution of her honorable claims on the general government, she was the object of the utmost veneration and affectionate wonder to all those who delighted to throng her modest dwelling, and hear from her eloquent, truthful lips, narratives of the times of which she was a part and an ornament.

Such was Mrs. Bethune's especial friend and longest loved associate in the rearing, establishing, and perpetuating the New York Orphan Asylum. Mrs. Hamilton continued to be the First Directress of the society until her removal to Washington, a few years before her death, when she was succeeded by Mrs.

Bethune. According to her dying request, Mrs. Hamilton's remains lie buried in Trinity Church-yard, near the tomb built for her illustrious husband by the Society of Cincinnati, whose President General (after Washington) he was. Among the most sincere and affectionate mourners at her funeral was my beloved mother.

The Rev. Dr. Weston (St. Paul's, New York), at the request of the Orphan Asylum Board, prepared a sermon eloquently commemorative of her many virtues and pious services, to be preached in the chapel of the institution, but was prevented by illness from delivering it.

CHAPTER XIV.

THE SUM OF HER LABORS, AND HER REST.

Review.—Mr. and Mrs. Bethune's Plans.—Visit of Missionaries.—
Church Relations. — Sunday-schools. — Economical School. —
House of Industry.—Instruction of the Young.—Mrs. Bethune's
Death.

[THE closing chapter of this memoir is taken from
a sketch which the Rev. Dr. Bethune prepared and
published immediately after the death of his mother.
He left the biography unfinished; and, in order to
complete it in his words, this sketch is here inserted,
though it repeats some facts already mentioned.—
Editor.]

Before the year 1807 Mr. Bethune and his very
intimate friend, Mr. Robert Ralston, of Philadelphia,
sympathizing in larger missionary views than those
generally entertained in this country at that time,
had made themselves Foreign Directors of the London Missionary Society, the only two such in the
United States. In 1807, that society sent to this
country (to avoid French cruisers), on his way to
China, the Rev. Mr. (afterward Dr.) Morrison, the
translator of the Bible into Chinese, and the Rev.
Messrs. Gordon and Lee, on their way to India.
These brethren, while waiting for a vessel, spent the
greater part of their time in Mr. Bethune's family,

with great spiritual advantage, as they afterward testified; and animated the pious three, Mrs. Graham, Mr. and Mrs. Bethune, with yet more ardent desires for promoting the Divine glory.

There was also another missionary who, for similar reasons, came to this country, on his way to India, and was intimate with the Bethune family—the Rev. Mr. May, of whom the writer can ascertain no more than that he was eminently distinguished by his love for children, whom he delighted to address, and by whom he was attended in large numbers. Mrs. Bethune used to express herself as having been greatly interested by Mr. May's efforts; and, from her own sayings, there is no doubt that her zeal for an instrumentality like the Sabbath-school was much increased. For several years after this Mrs. Bethune suffered much from ill health, but continued to maintain her charitable and religious engagements with great success; and, about the time when Dr. Mason removed his ministry to the new church built for him in Murray Street, Mr. and Mrs. Bethune and Mrs. Graham transferred their Church-membership to the Cedar Street Presbyterian Church, then under the pastoral care of the Rev. Dr. Romeyn; and of that church (after some intermediate changes, rendered necessary by changes in the city) Mrs. Bethune was a communicant at the time of her death, the attachment between her and her beloved pastor, Dr. James W. Alexander, having been of the most tender description.

About the year 1812 (the precise date can not now be given), the attention of Mr. and Mrs. Bethune was called to the blessed effects of the Sunday-school system established in England by Robert Raikes. Their pious correspondents in England, particularly Stephen Prust, Esq., of Bristol, sent them many reports and documents illustrating the work; and they endeavored to awaken the Christian public to that means of usefulness, but, for a time, with little success. Pious people, and some eminent ministers, even doubted the propriety of so occupying the Sabbath day. Mr. Bethune, weary of delay, at last said to Mrs. Bethune, "My dear wife, there is no use in waiting for the *men;* do you gather a few ladies of different denominations, and begin the work yourselves." Mrs. Bethune had already made encouraging experiments in two schools—one, during the winter, near her city residence, within convenient distance of Dr. Romeyn's church; the other in the basement of her country-seat, between Bank and Bethune Streets, Greenwich, besides starting others, as she had opportunity, during her summer travels in different parts of the country between the Hudson and the Lakes. Intent upon a wider diffusion of the blessing, she determined to call a public meeting of ladies, of different denominations, in the Wall Street Church, which she addressed from the clerk's desk; and, aided by many noble women, among whom may be noted Mrs. Francis Hall, of the Methodist, Mrs. William Colgate, of the Baptist, and Miss Ball, of the Dutch churches, she had the happiness of seeing put into successful operation "The Female Union for the Promotion of Sabbath-schools," which continued, by its publications and its schools, containing 7000 or 8000 children, to exert a large usefulness, until it was absorbed by the New York branch of the American Sunday-school Union. There had been Sunday-schools of various kinds, in various places, before this: Mrs. Graham, as early as 1792, had an adult Sunday evening school in Mulberry Street, and Mrs. Bethune, in subsequent years, had made several similar efforts; but this may be regarded as truly the first introduction here of the Raikes' system, as will be shown on some future occasion, when time is had for proper research.

Mrs. Bethune had a wise dread of administering charity in such a way as might encourage pauperism, and adopted fully the views of economists like Colquhoun on Indigence, Chalmers on Civic Economy of Large Towns. Of this she gave convincing proofs.

The war of 1812–14 brought great distress on the laboring classes, and the cry of the needy roused Mrs. Bethune to new energy for their relief. The great trouble was the scarcity of work. Mrs. Bethune, having duly considered the plan, associated herself with a number of like-minded ladies in a society for the promotion of industry. They rented a large wooden building, called The Economical School, then standing on the north side of Anthony (now Worth) Street,

F

a short distance from Broadway, west.   Here they
provided work for five or six hundred women, until
the urgent necessity passed away with the return of
peace.   Some idea of the enterprise and business talent with which the institution was managed may be
got from the fact that they successfully competed for
and fulfilled a contract with government to supply a
sloop-of-war, or a frigate, with all its necessary clothing, bed-clothes, etc., etc.   This House of Industry was
the model on which a similar institution in Boston,
and others elsewhere, were framed.   Mrs. Bethune,
some years afterward, endeavored to introduce the
plan recommended by Chalmers, of dividing the city
into districts, to be visited with such accuracy that no
dwelling of the poor should be neglected.   The plan
was, however, superseded by the system of the Association for the Relief of the Poor, since then so no-
bly carried out.

Mrs. Bethune's greatest delight was in the education of the young.   She loved education as a science
as well as a charity.   Hence she was always personally attentive to that department of the Orphan Asylum, and taught her Sabbath class until she had long
passed her eightieth year.   It is not surprising, therefore, that the infant-school system, as organized by
Wilderspin, on the basis of Pestalozzi's plan of development, should have deeply interested her.   On receiving the necessary books from England and Switzerland, she succeeded, May 23d, 1827, in establishing
a society for advancing that method of instruction,

aided by the late able philanthropist, John Griscom, and also by Mr. S. W. Seton, a devoted friend of youth. Several schools (at least nine) were put into successful operation, which Mrs. Bethune actively superintended, and one of them she taught herself, almost entirely, in the worst neighborhood of the Five Points—this more than thirty years ago. The infant-school plan was soon adopted as supplementary to the larger classes in Sunday-schools, and in the primaries of our public schools, so that the good thus begun has been, and will be, perpetuated on a more extended scale. Several books of infant-school instruction, written and edited by Mrs. Bethune, are still highly prized, and must long continue to help the teacher and the taught.

So crowded with incident and work was the life of Mrs. Bethune; and none can estimate the influence of her devoted life. But a few years since her aged, hard-worked brain showed symptoms of weakness, and she retired from active pursuits, to find tranquillity in the home of her son, who was permitted to receive her last breath. The last intelligible sentence that she uttered was, " All has been done well !" She sank to rest like a little child in its father's arms, without a struggle, a sign of suffering, or complaint, closing her own dear eyes, and, by her last voluntary muscular movement, composing her lips as she was wont to do when falling asleep. Her rest came after a long pilgrimage; but her works have followed her before the throne of Him in whom alone she trusted, and that rest is glorious.

APPENDIX.

EXTRACTS FROM THE PRIVATE PAPERS, JOURNALS, ETC., OF MRS. JOANNA BETHUNE.

A DAY OF SORROW.

New York, September 21st, 1824.

SEPTEMBER 18th, at eight o'clock in the evening, it pleased an all-wise God to take to Himself my beloved husband, and to write upon me, the happiest of wives, WIDOW. To this day I have never been able to look, and often thought I could not bear it; yet the day is come. The Lord has taken away the desire of my eyes with a stroke. Although I can not say that I neither mourn nor weep, nor that my tears do not run down, yet I am enabled to kiss the hand that smites, and to say, "Thy will be done." "The Lord gave, and the Lord hath taken away; blessed be the name of the Lord."

I desire to record the goodness of God to my dear husband, in making all his bed in his sickness, in placing underneath him the everlasting arms, in allowing him to lean upon his Master's bosom, and sweetly to fall asleep in Jesus, without an agonizing struggle, without even the movement of a muscle, hand or foot. And now the conflict is past. His work is done, and well done, and his longing desire is satisfied. "Let me go home. Let me go to my Savior. My race is run; my work is done. Let me go."

And now, O thou Infinite Jehovah, before whom I have been pouring out my soul by the bed upon which my beloved husband resigned his happy spirit, I claim Thy promise that Thou, my Maker, will be my husband, and counsel and direct me in every duty before me. I can no longer ask my husband, and receive aid and counsel from him, in every difficulty, as I have done for twenty-nine years; but if Thou lift upon me the light of Thy countenance, and make Thy Word a light to my feet and a lamp to my path, I can not err. I have now no idol to draw off my affections from Thee. My daughters find rest in the houses of their husbands. My son, if spared, will settle in life; but the widow will sit desolate. O grant, then, that I may be a widow indeed. Lord, Thou knowest the difficulties before me. Counsel, direct, and enable me to perform them all with a single eye to Thy glory. May I never disgrace Thy name, nor the name of him who is sleeping in the dust.

O Lord, while I ask the forgiveness of my trespasses, enable me to forgive others their trespasses. And now, Lord, this 21st of September, 1824, I solemnly devote myself to Thee, in my new character of widow, and claim all the promises to such in Thy precious Bible. I desire to sit desolate as to man, and to be presented as a chaste virgin unto Thee. I desire to glorify Thee in this hot furnace, to see Thy hand in my bereavement. Henceforth I devote myself to Thee—soul, body, and estate, all that I have, and all that I am. O, my covenant God, help me to be faithful to this dedication; and, as my blessed love told me, to live near to God. He told me I idolized him. I feel I did. But my idol Thou hast taken away; my gourd Thou hast withered. Lord, help me, or I perish.

O Lord, look on the children of Thy servant and Thy handmaid. Sanctify this affliction to them and to their children; and, when their father and their mother are sleeping in the dust, may they, as he said, do their parts, and all be gathered home at last, where all tears shall be wiped from our eyes, and where sorrow and sighing shall forever flee away. Amen. Come, Lord Jesus! come quickly!

Sabbath evening, October 3d, 1824.

O Lord, I am indeed in a new situation. Accustomed to lean upon the kindest, the tenderest of husbands, who provided for all my wants, who felt for all my troubles, who bore with my weaknesses and faults, and who, I fear, occupied the place in my heart which Thou only ought to fill; but now that Thou hast cut down my idol, Thou hast withered my gourd, I feel desolate. I have now not only the charge of managing property, and sworn that I will faithfully fulfill the trust reposed in me, but I have a mercantile concern to attend to, being sole heir and sole executrix, and my beloved husband having left no partner. Lord, help me in this trying season. I have had an example before me, to spread every thing before the Lord; of recording texts and promises, and pleading them in faith, and looking for the answer. I draw near to Thee, O my God, in present difficulties. Thou knowest them all. I will record some Scriptures, and leave them before Thee for Thy answer: the cxliii. Psalm throughout, viewing the enemies mentioned in it as spiritual enemies. Prov., iv., 11, 12, 13: Do Thou so to me, O Lord. O, do Thou teach me the way of wisdom, and lead me in right paths. When I go, let not my steps be straitened; and when I run, suffer me not to stumble. May I take fast hold of instruction, and keep her as my life. Isaiah, xli., 10: Fear not, for I am with thee; be not dismayed, for I am thy God. I will strengthen thee, I will help thee; yea, I will uphold thee with the right hand of my righteousness; v. 13: For I the Lord will hold thy right hand, saying unto thee, Fear not; I will help thee.

Sabbath, February 6, 1825.

Heb., xi., 1: Now faith is the substance of things hoped for, the evidence of things not seen. The whole chapter gives a clear view of the faith of the believer.

O, my gracious covenant God, I desire, on this

Thine own day, to draw near to Thy throne, to take a fresh hold of Thy covenant for myself, as Thy widowed handmaid, and for my fatherless children. " Leave thy fatherless children upon Me, and I will preserve them alive," was the promise Thou didst enable Thine aged handmaid to lay hold of and plead through a long life. Thou didst graciously hear and answer her prayer for her seed and her seed's seed, and Thou didst hear and answer the prayers of Thy dear servant, and didst give him faith in Thy Word for his seed. He was permitted to see all his children, I trust, taught of God. And now those two eminent saints have finished their course, and all their anxieties respecting their dear offsprings are over, while Thine unworthy handmaid, the least of all saints, remains behind, to supply their place to the dear children Thou didst give us. O Lord, now that their prayers no longer ascend in our behalf, may we be quickened to greater diligence in praying for ourselves!

And, O Lord, I would this afternoon, in an especial manner, come to Thee in behalf of Thy young servant, the son of Thine handmaid. O Lord, I thank Thee for restoring him to me in health and strength for a short season. I thank Thee—O, I adore Thee, for the grace in which he stands. I thank Thee that, in some degree, he has been made to see the insufficiency of the pleasures of this world to impart happiness. I thank Thee that Thou hast made him willing, in a day of Thy power, to turn his back on the city of destruction, and to set his face toward Zion. And I would now earnestly plead with Thee that Thou wouldst increase his faith, and give him more grace. O Lord, he has chosen the most responsible of all professions — a profession which Thou only canst fit him for. All that man can teach him will only bewilder, unless accompanied by the teaching of Thy Holy Spirit. O, pour out upon me, his only parent, a spirit of prayer and supplication in his behalf, and lead him to Thee in all difficulties, and ask wisdom. Open the eyes of his understanding, that he may see wondrous things in Thy law. He is now beginning to prepare discourses. Lord, impress upon his mind that the great object of his profession is to proclaim salvation through Christ to dying sinners. May he remember the dying words of his dear father, " Preach the Gospel, my son ! Tell dying sinners of a Savior ! Mind nothing else; it is all folly !" Give him clear views of doctrine, particularly of faith, which seems to puzzle him. O Lord, for Thy name's sake — for the sake of Him whom Thou hearest always—look upon my son, the only son of his mother, and she a widow ! Make him more spiritual, more self-denied, more devoted ! Give him some love-tokens that shall so take hold of his affections that he shall have more joy in serving Thee, and more happiness in waiting upon Thee, than the worldling " when his corn and his wine abound." O, grant him the grace of application and perseverance in searching the Scriptures; and may he never attempt the duty without crying unto Thee for Thy Holy Spirit to guide him unto all truth. Give him great grace; and let a double portion of the same Spirit that dwelt in his father rest upon him. Instead of the father, do Thou now take the son, and make him as eminently useful as a minister as Thou didst make him as an officer in Thy Church and as a layman. Lord, as Thou hast commanded, I open my mouth wide, and do Thou fill it. Answer all the prayers now before Thy throne for this dear youth, and lay him on the minds of thy dear people. Lead them to pray what Thou hast determined to grant, that he may be a faithful, humble, and able minister of the New Testament.

March 17, 1825.

In obedience to the command of God, and under a deep sense of my own incapacity to do any thing aright of myself, I come before God this day to plead with Him to hear and answer my petitions for myself, and my children, and children's children, in the view of my approaching dissolution. Before making my will, I ask of God the following great favors:

O, my God! the God of my father, the God of my mother, the God of my beloved and dearest of all earthly friends—the God of my husband—but, above all, the God and Father of the Lord Jesus Christ, I come this day to do as Thou directest; to set my house in order, knowing that assuredly I shall die, and not live. 1st. I ask that, during the remaining years, months, weeks, days, or hours I may live, I may, by Thy grace assisting me, walk before Thee with a perfect heart. 2d. That I may never disgrace Thy holy name, by which I am called, and that I may order all my affairs with discretion. 3d. That I may provide things honest and of good report in the sight of all men. 4th. That I may have a portion to give to the widow, the fatherless, the stranger, the sick and afflicted; and, if not too much to ask, that I may still be permitted to aid in institutions laboring for the spread of the Gospel and advancing the kingdom of my dear Redeemer, who has done so much for me and mine. 5th. That I may have a measure of health while I live, and be taken home to the mansion prepared for me by my Lord and Savior when I have done the work Thou hast assigned me on earth. If consistent with Thy holy will, that I may not be left to be a burden to myself and others. Nevertheless, not my will, but Thine be done. I desire to ask with submission. One thing more I ask, and would plead earnestly for, and ask my gracious Redeemer to intercede for me, that Thy sensible presence may be with me all the way when passing through the Valley of the Shadow of Death. O, may I hear the voice of Him saying, "Let not your heart be troubled; ye believe in God, believe also in me. In my Father's house are many mansions; if it were not so, I would have told you. I go to prepare a place for you. And if I go and prepare a place for you, I will come again, and receive you to myself; that where I am, there you may be also." Grant, if consistent with Thy holy will, that I may have an easy transition; that the enemy may not have permission to assault me; and that, like my dear mother and still dearer husband, I may lean on my Master's bosom, and sweetly fall asleep in Jesus. I ask all these favors, not for any worthiness in me, but for the sake of Him whom Thou hearest always. Amen. Come, Lord Jesus! come quickly! And now, Lord, for my children and children's children, I ask that they may indeed be ALL taught of God, to the latest generation. It is a large boon, but Thou hast commanded, " Open thy mouth wide, and I will fill it." Nothing is too hard for Thee. Giving does not impoverish Thee, nor withholding make Thee rich. Grant that none of them may ever bring disgrace upon their profession. Spare my beloved daughters to train up their children in Thy fear. May they be help-meets to thy servants. And, O my gracious Father, look on my beloved son, the only son of his mother, and she a widow; the son for whom his father prayed, and whom he lent unto the Lord all the days of his life. O grant him all needful grace. Open the eyes of his understanding to read the Scriptures; make him a workman in Thy cause that needeth not to be ashamed. May he indeed be a chosen vessel, whom the Lord will send to preach the Gospel! Lord, grant that, when he shall have a companion, she may be a King's daughter. Choose Thou for him, gra-

cious God, one that will be a help-meet for him, who
will train up her children to serve the God of their
fathers.   O, may the houses of my beloved children
be Bethels to the Lord!   May the morning and evening sacrifice continually ascend from their dwellings!
May all my children, in every generation, seek first
the kingdom of God and His righteousness, and then
they have the promise that all temporal blessings necessary in this life Thou wilt add!   May the God before whom my fathers walked, the God before whom
your dear beloved father walked, and before whom
(oh how imperfectly) your mother has walked—the
God which fed me all my life long unto this day—the
Angel which redeemed me from all evil, bless you,
and let His name, even the name of the Lord Jesus
Christ, be named on you in all your generations; and
may you grow into a multitude in the midst of the
earth!   Of you and of your seed may it be said, in
every age, in answer to your father's prayers, and
for the sake of his God, "These are they who bring
the sacrifices of praise into the house of the Lord."
This was his prayer and hope for you, and this is my
prayer and hope for you: "Riches of grace in the covenant of Jehovah, more precious than the mines of
Golconda or Peru."   Amen and amen.

———◆———

March 18th, 1825.

The birthday of my beloved son George, now the
only son of his mother, and she a widow. Oh the

joy that this day twenty years was experienced by his beloved father and now desolate mother that a man-child was born into our family! His dear father, now in glory, prayed thus for him, after magnifying the Lord for His goodness, to his Maker in the trying hour: "Thou knowest that I have all along asked of my God that, if he gave us a son, that he might be sanctified from the womb, and be made a faithful, honored, and zealous minister of the everlasting Gospel. Lord, hear us in this thing." Then follow the texts: 1 Samuel, i., 27, 28. This I took March 14th; 1 Samuel, i., 23; Isaiah, lxv., 23, 24; Jeremiah, v., 5. All these promises he saw accomplished. When leaving his son at the Theological Seminary, oh how he sang praises to God, exultingly saying, "He worships the Lord there." Many of our Christian friends looked with amazement at the goodness of God toward our family, and gave glory to God in our behalf. "Now lettest Thou Thy servant depart in peace, for mine eyes have seen Thy salvation," was the language of both our hearts. Often, when meditating on the great happiness of our family (all our children being now taught of God), has my heart been ready to burst with gratitude to Him who had now answered all our prayers. Alas! little did I think that, in less than one year, this happy dwelling would be filled with lamentation and woe, and that, indeed, thy faithful servant would depart in peace. A *very few* months I could say I had not a wish ungratified.

"Like Jonah (well our stories suit),
　I viewed my gourd well pleased;
Like him, I could not see the root
　On which the worm had seized.

" But saw, at length, the hour draw nigh
　(That hour I since have known),
When he, my earthly joy, must die,
　And I be left alone.

" Now, Lord, I would to Thee apply,
　On Thee alone depend;
Thou art, when creatures fail and die,
　An ever-living friend !"

Many are the prayers, before Thy throne, offered by his dear grandmother and dear, dear father. O gracious God, answer them now; now let Thy blessing descend upon him. They, perhaps, are now looking down upon the poor afflicted widow weeping before Thee this day; her heart bleeding under Thy stroke, yet enabled to glorify Thee in the furnace, saying,

"Sharp was my pain, and deep my wound—
　A wound that still must bleed;
But daily help and strength I found,
　Proportioned to my need."

O gracious God, I desire now to return from the world, to be shut up with Thee, to plead Thy promises in behalf of my beloved son, this day twenty years old. I go to Thy Word to search for promises for him; direct me to them, O my God.

Psalm lxxxi., 10: I am the Lord which brought thee out of the land of Egypt: open thy mouth wide, and I will fill it. Acts, ii., 17: " And it shall come to pass in the last days, saith God, that I will pour out of my Spirit upon all flesh; and your sons and your daughters, shall prophesy;" and verse 21: "And it shall come to pass, that whosoever shall call on the name of the Lord shall be saved." Acts, ix., 15: "Go thy way; for he is a chosen vessel unto me, to bear my name before the Gentiles, and kings, and the children of Israel." Isaiah, lxiv., 1: Oh that Thou wouldst rend the heavens, that Thou wouldst come down, that the mountains might flow down at Thy presence; verse 4: For since the beginning of the world men have not heard, nor perceived by the ear, neither hath the eye seen, O God, beside Thee, what He hath prepared for him that waiteth for Him. Thou meetest him that rejoiceth and worketh righteousness, those that remember Thee in Thy ways; verse 6: But we are all as an unclean thing, and all our righteousnesses are as filthy rags; and we all do fade as a leaf; and our iniquities, like the wind, have carried us away; verse 8: But now, O Lord, Thou art our Father; we are the clay, and Thou our potter; and we are all the work of Thy hand; verse 9: Be not wroth very sore, O Lord, neither remember iniquity forever: behold, see, we are all Thy people. Jeremiah, i., 5: Before I formed thee in the belly I knew thee, and before thou camest forth out of the womb I sanctified thee, and I ordained thee a prophet unto the nations. Jeremiah, xxiv., 7: "And I will give them a heart to know me, that I am the Lord; and they shall be my people, and I will be their God; for they shall return unto me with their whole heart." Lord, fulfill this promise to our whole family! 1 Peter, ii., 5: "Ye also, as lively stones, are built up a spiritual house, a holy priesthood, to offer up spiritual sacrifices, acceptable to God by Jesus Christ;" verse 9: "But ye are a chosen generation, a royal priesthood, a holy nation, a peculiar people; that ye shall show forth the praises of Him who hath called you out of darkness into His marvelous light." Hebrews, iv., 16; v., 1, 2, 3, 4; vi., 19: "Which hope we have as an anchor of the soul, both sure and steadfast, which entereth into that within the vail." Joshua, i., 9: "Have not I commanded thee? Be strong and of good courage; be not afraid, neither be thou dismayed; for the Lord thy God is with thee whithersoever thou goest."

O most gracious God, fulfill the above to my beloved son. O grant me faith to lay hold on the promises for him. Grant him faith to lay hold on them for himself. O may he plead with Thee, for his Redeemer's sake, for sanctification; and may he daily grow in grace and in the knowledge of the Lord his God. Bless abundantly, also, my sons-in-law in their calling. Keep me, keep my sons, keep my children and grandchildren pure and unspotted from the world.

> "Guide us, O Thou great Jehovah,
> Pilgrims through this barren land;
> We are weak, but Thou art mighty;
> Hold us with thy powerful hand.
> Bread of Heaven,
> Feed us till we want no more."

Amen.   Come, Lord Jesus.

> "When I tread the verge of Jordan,
>   Bid our anxious fears subside;
> Foe to death, and Hell's destruction,
>   Land us safe on Canaan's side.
>   Songs of praises
>   We will ever give to Thee."

Hallelujah! the Lord God Omnipotent reigneth.

May 1st, 1825.

The last night I have to spend under the roof where my beloved husband poured out his soul to Thee, O Lord, and where, in answer to his prayer, he leaned upon his Master's bosom while passing through the valley of the shadow of death. O look down upon me to strengthen me, support me. O go with me, or carry me not up hence. Enable me yet to glorify Thee; make me useful in the neighborhood to which I am going. Lord, pardon my unfaithfulness to those around me here. O Lord, when I review my past life, even since I professed to follow Thee, my sins rise up in frightful array before me. Oh, wert Thou to mark iniquity, who could stand! I can not look on a single act of my life that was not defiled with sin; and what can I say but the prayer of the publican, "Lord, be merciful to me a sinner!"

I this night enter my record in this book that, if I am saved from hell, and shall have the unspeakable happiness of taking possession of a mansion prepared for me by my dear Redeemer, it will be all of grace, free and unmerited grace, and not for any filthy rags of righteousness of mine.

> " Oh to grace how great a debtor
> Daily I'm constrained to be ;
> Let that grace, Lord, like a fetter,
> Bind my wandering heart to Thee."

September 18, 1825.

The anniversary of the departure of my earthly joys, and the dismission of my beloved husband's happy spirit from sin and sorrow. One year of happiness to him, and one of sore, sore trial to me, his bereaved widow. What has been my experience through life but "cease from man, whose breath is in his nostrils?" But I knew not the full import of the text while I had my beloved husband to lean upon. My little trials diminished when poured into his affectionate bosom ; and when I was cheered and counseled by him in my Christian course, or in my labors in the societies, difficulties disappeared. True, I waited upon God, attempted no duty without first asking counsel of Him, but never till now did I know what it is to trust the naked promise, and feel that loneliness which throws the heart back on itself— that complete destitution of human aid. Whenever I have leaned on the creature, be it who it will, I have found it a broken reed ; and often, even those whom I have considered my best friends have proved spears

to pierce me to the heart. "This is not your rest,"
is legibly written on all below. All my cisterns are
broken.

> " Vain is the world, and all things here;
>   'Tis but a bitter sweet:
> When I attempt a rose to pluck,
>   A pricking thorn I meet."

And what has been the language of God's providence to me during the past year? The same as formerly. "Cease from man." "Wherefore will you
spend your money for naught, and your labor for that
which satisfieth not?" "Come unto me, all ye that
labor and are heavy laden, and *I* will give you rest.
Learn of me, for I am meek and lowly." God will
admit of no rivals. He will take them one by one,
till He has the whole heart; and it ought to make us
tremble, when we look for comfort to the creature,
that God, when we pray, will answer us according to
the multitude of our idols. This is, no doubt, why I
remain so rebellious—why I still hanker after the
sympathy of friends, and feel hurt when they neglect,
or do not seem to feel for me, till I am constrained to
cry out with the prophet, "Woe is me for my hurt!
my wound is grievous; but I said, truly this is my
grief, and I must bear it." There is no avoiding it.
None *will*, none *can* help me but God. Would that
I acted in consistency with this belief, and looked to
Him alone. Would that I cast my burden on the
Lord, believing that He would sustain me, and not
continually attempt to lay it on my own or the crea-

ture's shoulders. As I had not a thought unknown to my beloved husband, and cared for no sympathy but his, why do I not act in the same way toward my Maker, who condescends to call himself my husband, and to whom I married and devoted myself, soul, body, and estate, the day after my creature husband was laid in the grave? "And I said, I will not transgress;" yet how often have I wandered from Him, playing the harlot! As a wife treacherously departeth from her husband, so have I treacherously departed from my heavenly Husband. "It is of the Lord's mercies that I am not consumed, because His compassions fail not."

I confess this day before *Thee*, my God, that I have broken all my resolutions; that I have not been faithful to my vows, but have transgressed times and ways without number. I have too often poured my complaint into the creature's ear, and have not often enough, nor conscientiously enough, entered into my closet, and prayed to my heavenly Father. I have not listened to the voice of my Redeemer. I have, indeed, bemoaned myself like Ephraim, as a bullock unaccustomed to the yoke; but I have not meekly submitted to my lot, nor kissed the rod. The fruit of my affliction has not been to take away sin. I have not been properly exercised, and therefore it has not yielded the peaceable fruit of righteousness. O Lord, I experience daily that the way of man is not in himself. It is not in man that walketh to direct his steps. "O Lord, correct me, but with judgment;

not in Thine anger, lest Thou bring me to nothing."
—Jer., x., 23–4. To whom can I go but unto Thee?
I come, Lord, vile, polluted, hell-deserving sinner as I
am, loathing and abhorring myself, and repenting in
dust and ashes! Oh, may I hear Thy voice saying,
"Turn, thou backsliding daughter, for I am married
unto you!" Betroth me to Thyself in an everlasting
covenant. Suffer me never again to cherish an evil
heart of unbelief in departing from the living God.
"Lord, help me, or I perish!" Oh, may the year to
come find me more faithful to my vows—more conscientious in performing all my duties; more humble,
more meek and lowly, more forbearing toward others. Set a fresh watch upon my lips, that I offend
not with my tongue. May I "lay aside every weight,
and the sin which most easily besets me, and run
with patience the race that is set before me, looking
continually to Jesus, who is the author and finisher
of my faith." I desire to take a fresh hold of my covenant, ordered in all things and sure, for myself, my
children, my children's children, my sons-in-law, and
dear Mary, the chosen of my son. Oh grant that we
may all be guided *here* by Thy counsel, and hereafter
received to Thy glory. Bless and reward all my
friends; pardon my enemies, and enable me to forgive
them, and cherish no bitterness against them; but
may my prayer still be for them in their calamities.
I leave me upon Thee. Do what seemeth Thee good
with me, only take not Thy Holy Spirit from me,
but hold me up continually by Thy right hand.

To God my Father and Husband, to God my crucified and risen Savior, and to God the Holy Spirit, who comforteth me in all my afflictions, be glory forever and ever. Amen.

My son, my last born and only child remaining unmarried, is united to another in the tenderest connection, which nothing but death can dissolve. And now, indeed, I feel alone as to the creature. My daughters find rest in the houses of their husbands. They keep at home, bring up their children, and, of course, as I did myself (oh how delightful), find their happiness in their own families. My son has now left his widowed mother, and cleaves to his wife.

It seems as if my work was done. Why am I spared? I come to Thee, O my heavenly Father, to ask the question. Thou Friend, that sticketh closer than a brother! Thou Husband of the widow! Thou Father of the fatherless! Thou Shield of the stranger! Thou Stay of the orphan, I claim Thee in all these characters, for I am a widow, fatherless, a stranger, and an orphan. Oh, then, calm the tumult of my mind. Thou canst be better to me than father, mother, husband, children. Show me then, O my God, why Thou sparest me, and what Thou wouldst have me to do. Make the path of duty plain before me. May I continue to hear a voice behind me, saying, "This is the way; walk ye in it." However trying to flesh and blood, enable me to take up my cross daily. Oh that I could indeed rest in God!

I have been looking over some of my beloved's letters of 1800. Oh how closely he walked with God, and how sweetly did he comfort me by pointing out precious promises and texts to encourage me to pray over them. Twenty-five years ago, when harassed by trials, no doubt trying to flesh and blood, but which now seem trifles in comparison to those heavy trials I have since passed through, he mentioned the 17th and 18th verses of James iii., and, as an encouraging promise, James, i., 5. No doubt I prayed over them then; and now I find the same spirit in me, and again I have been praying for deliverance from a murmuring temper. So true is it that the Canaanites shall not cease out of the land, but the Lord will drive them out by little and little; and not till the last breath be drawn shall we cease to be troubled with a body of sin and death. Lord, Thou seest how little progress I have made in the Divine life. I am the same murmuring, rebellious creature I was twenty-five years ago. O Lord, look on me in mercy. May I yet live to Thy praise. May I bring forth fruit in old age, if I have not in youth. On the topmost bough may there be some fruit found. Why do I still grovel below, and why do I not pant more after conformity to Thine image. Whom have I now to lean upon? *Not one.* Many look to me for help, but who is there to help me? Oh, then, enable me to look to Thee alone, Thou Friend of the friendless!

G

"Thou, O Christ, art all I want;
Freely let me take of Thee;
Spring Thou up within my heart;
Rise to all eternity."

The 86th and 88th Psalms suit me at present.
"Lover and friend hast Thou put far from me, and my
acquaintance in darkness; but Thou art a God full
of compassion and gracious, long-suffering, and plen-
teous in mercy and truth. O turn unto me, and have
mercy upon me. Give Thy strength unto Thy servant and the son of Thy handmaid. Show me a token
for good, that they which hate me may see it and be
ashamed; because Thou, Lord, hast holpen me and
comforted me. Teach me Thy way, O Lord. I will
walk in Thy truth. Unite my heart to fear Thy
name." Amen. Come, Lord Jesus! come quickly!

March 21st, 1826.

This evening I expect a few religious friends, to
converse on the subject of infant schools. I have
often thought on the subject, and have prayed to the
Lord, if it was His will, to use me as an instrument
in promoting them, and now he seems about to answer my prayer. Why, oh why am I thus honored?
"Even so, Father, for so it seemeth good in Thy
sight." Thou art never at a loss for an instrument
when Thou hast work to do. Thou often choosest
the weak things of this world to confound the wise.
O may the time be come when we shall begin at the
root—when the first lisping accents of babes shall be

heard in praising Thy name. Look now on Thy widowed handmaid before Thee, married to Thee, and devoted to Thy service from the day Thou didst take away the desire of my eyes with a stroke. My beloved mother told me, on her death-bed, to give myself to the young; and from the time that I did so, Thou hast given me pleasant work to do, and hast not withheld from me my wages. Thou hast abundantly prospered the Orphan Asylum Society and Sabbath-schools; is it too much to ask Thee to give me to see the infant schools established, and some work for me to do in them? Lord, hear my prayer, now that I have retired to my room to plead Thy precious promises to Thine own people, and to pray for grace to follow the direction in Thy Word—that Word which has been and is, indeed, a light to my feet and a lamp to my path. I record the texts which I plead before Thee in behalf of the work we are to set about this evening: Proverbs, iii., 5, 6; Psalm xxxvii., 5; Genesis, xxiv., xxvii., 4; Psalm xxvii., 11; Exodus, xxxiii., 13–18.

Lord, I come boldly unto a throne of grace, to obtain mercy and find grace for a time of need. Thou hast commanded, "Open thy mouth wide, and I will fill it." Lord, I obey. I open my mouth wide. I ask nothing less than that all may be taught of God to know Thee, the true God, "from the least unto the greatest." Must not that time come? Yea, we know it shall come; and, as the Lord works by means, may the little company to meet here this evening be the instruments who are to bring about the fulfillment of thy prophecies!

Rockaway, L. I., July 4, 1826.

My dear children are all now at this place, in Providence, after an absence of nine years, and I am now a desolate widow. Oh, how many recollections crowd on my mind while again revisiting this place. O Lord, remember not against me former iniquities. Let Thy tender mercies speedily prevent me, for I am brought very low. Help us, O God of our salvation, for the glory of Thy name, and deliver us, and purge away our sins, for Thy name's sake; so we, the people of Thy pasture, will give Thee thanks forever. We will show forth Thy praise to all generations. Turn us again, O God of Hosts, and cause Thy face to shine, and we shall be saved; upon us, Thy widowed handmaid and the children whom Thou hast given her, all Thy professing people, and one a minister of the Gospel. "Let Thy hand be upon the man of Thy right hand—upon the man whom Thou madest strong for Thyself; so will we not go back from Thee. Quicken us, and we will call upon Thy name." But, O gracious God, give us all, each one for himself and for herself, to ask in faith for that quickening Spirit. Much, much have I to repent of before Thee; and never till now have I appreciated the anxiety and prayers of my widowed mother; yet, Lord, to whom can I go but to Thee? Thou, and

Thou only, canst pardon; Thou, and Thou only, canst comfort me; Thou, and Thou only, canst sustain me amid my various trials and difficulties. My chief anxiety at present, O Lord, Thou knowest, is for my beloved son, " the only son of his mother, and she a widow"—this son, for whom his father prayed, and lent to the Lord for all the days of his life. Like Abraham, he saw the promise afar off. O grant the answer to the prayer of faith, which often and often he presented at Thy throne in his behalf, and may *now* be the time to answer all the prayers of twenty-one years. Lord, I tremble to think that the least of the three who united in dedicating this son should be left to witness the answer of part of the prayers put up for him, even to hear him preach—that I only have resting upon me the responsibilities of a *parent.* O Lord, grant me now that wisdom which is profitable to direct me in the path of duty. Let me not hesitate to admonish and warn him, and advise him; and do Thou give him that charity which endureth all things, and that spirit of meekness under reproof which he will have to preach to others. O Lord, grant that a double portion of the Spirit which rested on his dear father may rest on him. Let him not be negligent, seeing, I humbly trust, Thou hast chosen him to minister to Thee. O that he would hearken unto Thee, and walk in thy ways; then Thou hast promised that Thou wilt subdue his enemies, and turn Thy hand against his adversaries, even the corruptions of his heart, and especially the sin which most easily besets him, which Thou knowest.

I desire, this 14th day of July, 1826, to renew my covenant with Thee, my gracious Father, Savior, and Sanctifier, for myself and for my children, now fatherless. I have been pouring out my heart to Thee, confessing my own sins, and Thy right to chastise me for them. I again put my hand upon the head of the Lamb that was slain for sinners, confessing my sins and the sins of my children. As Thy people of old looked to the serpent that was lifted up in the wilderness, so now I desire to look, for myself and my children, to the lifted-up Healer, the blessed Jesus; and as the children of Israel were healed of their dreadful diseases, so may we be healed of the more dreadful maladies of *sin*. Grant that, as the scapegoat fled away with the sins of the people, my sins and the sins of my children may be blotted out from the book of Thy remembrance. The blood of Christ cleanses from *all* sin. Take us then, O Lord, as a family called by Thy name; a family to whom Thy steppings have been very stately; in whom are witnessed the answers of many prayers, the prayers of faith, put up by those who have now taken possession of the mansions prepared for them, from whose eyes Thou hast wiped away all tears, and who are now seated at Thy right hand, where they shall enjoy pleasures unalloyed for evermore. Yet a little while, when we have finished the work Thou hast laid out for us, may we also, through grace, join with them in singing the song of the Redeemer. O enable me to be willing to wait all the days of my appointed time, till my change come; and instead of the fathers and mothers, do Thou take the children, and cause them to walk still more circumspectly in the way of Thy commandments than ever we have done, and to be much more useful in their day and generation than we have been, and to be the honored instruments of advancing the kingdom of that dear Savior who has done so much for them.

New York, Sabbath evening, July 15th, 1826.

This day my son preached his first sermon in a regular church (my son M'Cartee's). The Lord was very gracious to him, and carried him through with great ease to himself; and, I have reason to think, his discourse was acceptable. His text was, Galatians, vi., 14: "But God forbid that I should glory, save in the cross of Christ." Glory to God, who has this day answered the prayers of twenty-one years. The following texts were given me this morning for my comfort, and which I now record as answered by my compassionate High-Priest, in carrying my beloved son through, and giving me composure of mind while hearing him: Psalm xxxviii., 15: For in Thee, O Lord, do I hope: Thou wilt hear, O Lord my God. Forsake me not, O Lord; O my God, be not far from me. Make haste to help me, O God of my salvation. Daniel, ix., 17, 18, 19: Now therefore, O our God, hear the prayer of Thy servant, and *our* supplications, and cause Thy face to shine upon Thy sanctuary that is desolate, for the Lord's sake. O my God, incline Thine ear and hear; open Thine eyes, and behold our desolations. We are a family called by Thy name; for we do not present our supplications before Thee for our righteousness, but for Thy great mercies. O Lord, hear; O Lord, forgive; O Lord, hearken and do; defer not, for Thine own sake, O my God; for we are a people called by Thy name. Bless the Lord, O my soul! Halleluiah! Amen. And now, Lord, Thou hast heard and answered all our prayers for this youth, in giving me to see him a herald of the Cross; but, O Lord, unless Thy presence accompany him in his labors, let him not go a step farther. But let not my faith fail at this late period, after trusting and believing so long. He who has begun the good work will carry it on to the day of Christ Jesus. In Thy hands I leave him, O my covenant God. Thou hast, and Thou wilt do all things well.

I will now record some providential circumstances connected with this important period of my son's life. Nine years ago I was at Rockaway, with my daughters, and we were the means of establishing a Sabbath-school there. The school-house being too small to accommodate all the scholars, and Mrs. Cornell wishing also to have a place where ministers could come and preach occasionally, got me to write a petition for a block-house that was going to decay. The petition was granted. Mr. Cornell gave ground to set it in; the neighbors volunteered, with their teams, to move it, and subscriptions were collected to make quite a decent place of worship on the Sabbath, as well as Sabbath-school. Since that period they have had frequent preaching in it. I have never been there since until last week. I was not anxious for George to go, lest the company might dissipate his mind, after the solemn exercises he had been engaged in while passing trials for licensure; but—oh the goodness of God—the night we arrived there a minister was to preach, but, being very ill, asked George if he was licensed, and if he would take his place. Thus, in the *house* which our family had been the means of getting, my dear son preached his first sermon. He also had family worship morning and evening, at which nearly all the boarders attended; and thus, at the very outset of his ministry, he was called to show his zeal for the Lord, in accordance with the first hymn he gave out,

"I'm not ashamed to own my Lord," etc.

I was much pleased with his conduct during the few days we staid, and it was the more gratifying to me as the answers to my earnest prayers. For some time past he has occupied my mind almost entirely, being the subject of my thoughts and prayers after lying down and before rising up. Now, Lord, I once more cast myself and my children on *Thee*. Perfect what concerns us; give us all grace to persevere in well-doing; and oh! through the instrumentality of this youth's preaching, add to Thy Church many of such as shall be saved. Bless my dear sons-in-law.

G 2

Reward them both for their kindness to their fatherless brother. Continue to be the Husband of the widow and the Father of the fatherless, for in Thee do we hope. Amen.

New York, September 18th, 1826.

"A day to be remembered;" yes, a day to be remembered—the second anniversary of the dismissal from sin and sorrow of my beloved husband; the day when the Lord saw fit, in His all-wise and just providence, to take away the desire of my eyes. Two years of happiness to him; oh, must I still say, unhappiness to me? Yes; my tears still flow, and flow faster and more frequently than when first bereaved. The feeling of missing the right hand will remain while I am in the body. I have shut myself up to spend the day with my heavenly Husband. I have, on my knees, endeavored to recollect and confess the sins of the past year, and I have also endeavored to call to mind the many mercies of the past year. They, like my sins, are more in number than I can tell. O Thou who seest the bitter anguish of my heart, pardon my ingratitude, and deal not with me as my iniquities deserve but in wrath remember mercy. O give me rest from days of sad adversity, and may that rest be in *Thee*. While Thou emptiest me from vessel to vessel, pour into my heart those consolations which the world can not give (oh, do I not know it by sad experience?), and which, bless the

Lord, O my soul! the world can not take away. Although I never can, nor do I wish to forget, for a moment, my beloved husband, I would desire to look more to the mercies and blessings which remain, and for this purpose would enumerate the mercies of last year, and endeavor, by that means, to calm the tumult which, in spite of myself, almost overwhelms me. My tears flow till my head and my eyes ache, and my heart is like to break with the thought that I am indeed a desolate widow; that I never more can go to my beloved husband, and pour all my griefs and sorrows into his affectionate bosom; that I must plod my weary way *alone* through the wilderness; that he is no longer here to counsel me in difficulty and soothe me in trouble. I have been shutting myself up to spend the day with my Husband God; but his dear image continually presents itself to my mind —his sweet, benevolent countenance, as it were, smiles on me, and I have not resolution to put him aside, that I may commune with my God. Lord, help me! Take the place Thyself. Oh, bless me with Thine own unclouded day, and then I shall not miss the dying lamp which Thou hast removed.

March 18th, 1827—George's birthday. }
This day twenty-two years old.

My beloved son is at present in Savannah. I have been pouring out my heart to my covenant God in behalf of this dear youth, and pleading the promises selected by his dear father on the day of his birth and the day of his baptism, as also reading, praying, and weeping over many other papers also marked, in subsequent years, by the dear hand now mouldering in the dust. But I feel cold and listless, and need especially the influences of the Holy Spirit to thaw and melt my frozen heart. Oh, when I review the way in which the Lord has led me—when I read and recollect the many petitions he has granted, and the many mercies I ungratefully enjoy—I feel, indeed, that I ought, if I do not, loathe myself, and repent in dust and ashes for my ingratitude, and my doings which are not good. Every thing I asked this day two years for my son and myself the Lord has granted, as it respects temporal things, and, in some degree, spiritual. What can I say for all this exuberant goodness? *Nothing.* Not unto us, not unto us be the glory. It is all of grace, and grace shall have the praise.

> " Oh to grace how great a debtor
>   Daily I'm constrained to be ;
>   Let that grace, Lord, like a fetter,
>   Bind my wandering heart to Thee.
>
> " Prone to wander, Lord, I feel it ;
>   Prone to leave the God I love ;
>   Here's my heart—oh, take and seal it—
>   Seal it for Thy courts above."

Sabbath evening, March 26, 1827.

As I am about putting up a tablet to the memory of my dear beloved husband and mother in Pearl Street Church, under which the dear remains rest, I appointed to meet Mr. Strong on Friday evening, to fix upon a suitable place for it. It was preparation sermon. The Rev. Mr. Monteith, the pastor, preached from Psalm cxxvi., 6. It was a plain, practical discourse, and suited to my feelings, which were very tender. Many tender recollections connected with the place crowded on my mind. Mr. Monteith gave an invitation to members in good standing in sister churches who might be present to come forward and receive tokens of admission to the Lord's Supper the ensuing Sabbath. I accepted the invitation, and have this day again been at the table of the Lord. The subject of discourse was Heb., ii., 10 : " For it became Him, for whom are all things, and by whom are all things, in bringing many sons unto glory, to make the Captain of their salvation perfect through sufferings." I was fed, I think, both under the sermon and at the table; but oh, I fear the creature too often usurped the place of the Creator. So many associations with the place brought former scenes of joys and sorrows to my mind, that my eyes poured forth torrents of tears over departed relations; yet I trust I was not entirely without the kindlings of repentance when I reviewed my past life. Oh, it is a sad review ! What have I done during thirty-six years that I have been a communicant in the Church? Nothing! nothing! What would become of me if I had not a complete Savior—if the Captain of my salvation had not been made perfect through suffering? During the happy, happy years of my married life, I did not do as my beloved husband did, keep books of communion with my God, and now I feel the want. Sometimes I feel as if I had never enjoyed communion with Him, but all the past seems like a pleasing, and often painful dream; yet hundreds of instances crowd on my remembrance of answers to prayers put up at the Lord's table. Great encouragement I have had to pray in faith, although I have not recorded it. The *one* thing I asked for my children has been granted, and oh how much added! but the Lord had no sooner granted all the desires of our hearts respecting them than He began to weaken my beloved in the way, and now I am left alone of those who communicated in the church where two of three now rest. Now what is my petition this day? What remains for me to do? Have I still years before me, or am I shortly to follow those who have gone before? Are my days to glide heavily, but peacefully along to the grave, or have I to pass through still more tribulation before I enter the kingdom? Ah! Lord, Thou knowest. The Lord has done and finished all things well for those dear to me, and why should I not trust Him to do for me what seemeth good? "Lord, I believe; help my unbelief." Enable me this night to renew the covenant which Thou didst make

with me in youth. How often hast Thou drawn me
with the cords of love! How often hast thou laid
me on a sick-bed, and chastised me in other ways, to
bring me back to Thee when wandering from Thee;
but oh! nothing completely weaned me from the
world till Thou didst "take the desire of my eyes
with a stroke," and now I see I can have no enjoy-
ment more below, but as I enjoy it in the presence of
my Husband, God. Come, then, Lord, take complete
possession of my heart; make it indeed a temple of
the Holy Spirit. O drive out the buyers and sellers.
Purify all my motives, and hallow all my affections.
If it be Thy will to spare me years or months, give
me my work, and let me do it to Thee alone.

None can help me but God. I can not even take
the remedy offered unless He bid me stretch out the
withered hand. I can not pray unless He pour out
a spirit of prayer and supplication. I can not keep
my tongue from offending unless He set a watch upon
my lips. I can not see the path of duty unless He
anoint my eyes to see it. I can not even cast my
burden on the Lord unless His grace enable me.
The whole head is sick, the whole heart is faint;
from the crown of my head to the soles of my
feet, I am nothing but wounds, and bruises, and pu-
trefying sores. I am like an owl in the desert—a
pelican in the wilderness. I feel empty of every
thing; and if ever again I experience happiness in
this world—if ever again I am made to be useful—
if ever again I am favored with that peace that pass-

eth all understanding—if ever again I can say "my Beloved is mine and I am His"—if ever again I feel entire submission and acquiescence to the will of God—if ever again these weak, dying embers of grace in my heart be fanned into a flame, God must do it, and He only shall have *the praise*. Whatever others may say of moral ability, I am sure I have none. God must offer; God must give grace to accept. *He* must make me willing in a day of His power *now*, as the first time I believed. Lord, I lie at Thy mercy. Bid me come unto Thee, and I will come over these troubled waves, which threaten to overwhelm me. I leave myself in Thy hands. I can not doubt that I have once experienced Thy love shed abroad in my heart, and must still trust that Thou wilt yet have mercy upon me. Like Jonah, I will look again unto Thy holy temple. Blessed Word of God, what would I do without it? Only let the Spirit of the Lord shine on His own Word, and I can never be in darkness. Why art thou cast down, O my soul; I shall yet praise Him. Lord, do as Thou hast said. When I put Thee in remembrance, blot out my transgressions, for Thy name's sake, and remember no more my sins. O plead for me, my Savior! Show Thy hands and Thy feet pierced for me, and enable me again to say, My Lord and my God!

Sabbath, July 8, 1827.

This day I have again enjoyed the privilege of sitting down at the Lord's table, and eating and drinking the memorials of His broken body and shed blood. Mr. M'Cartee preached from John, i., 14: "And the Word was made flesh, and dwelt among us, and we beheld His glory, the glory of the Only-begotten of the Father, full of grace and truth." I trust I felt it a privilege to understand the meaning of the text, and to follow the Lord's servant through his discourse with the assent of my mind, but my heart was cold, and my desires after communion with my God very languid. My tears ought to have flowed for my sins, and the sorrows my Savior endured for these sins; but the fountains were sealed till he began to mention the departure of dear friends since last communion, and that he had never yet dispensed a sacrament that he did not miss some one that had sat down with us at the previous one; but I was overwhelmed when he quoted my beloved husband's dying words: "How can I doubt, how can I fear, when the eternal God is my refuge, and underneath me are the everlasting arms?" in contrast to the words of a dying sinner, "I can not die; oh, I can not die, sir! How can I face my God, whom I have despised?" Then, then the torrents poured forth; then the dear departed took the place the Savior ought to have held, and his countenance was again before me as on his dying bed, or as when in health, and looking upon my sorrow. Oh, still, still the idol! Still, still I hug the withered gourd. Lord, help me, or I perish! Looking for something to read, I laid my hand on Thomas à Kempis. I recollected it was a favorite book during the first year of my mother's widowhood, and there I found something to suit me. I here translate it for my future comfort, when exposed to the same temptations:

CHAPTER XLV.

"Against extravagant dejection upon being sometimes betrayed by human weakness.

"1st. Humility and patience, my son, under adversity, are more acceptable to me than much joy and fervor when all is prosperous without and peaceful within.

"2d. Why art thou offended and grieved at every little injury from men, when, if it were much greater, it ought to be borne without emotion? As fast as such evils arise, let their influence be banished from the mind. They are not new; thou hast met with many, and, if thy life be long, thou shalt meet with many more.

"3d. When adversity stands not in thy path, thou boastest of thy fortitude, and canst give excellent counsel to others, whom thou expectest to derive strength from thy exhortations; but no sooner do the same evils that oppressed them burn upon thyself, than thy fortitude forsakes thee, and thou art destitute both of counsel and of strength."

Lord, I confess it, it is so. I am, indeed, what Thou sayest, destitute of strength and counsel; and now I desire, in the words of the disciple replying to Christ, to say, "Thy words, O Lord, distill as the dew, and are sweeter to my taste than honey or the honey-comb." What would become of me, in the midst of so much darkness, corruption, and misery, without Thy Holy Spirit to illuminate, sanctify, and comfort me? I will not regard what or how much I suffer, if I can but be made capable of enjoying Thee, my supreme and only good. Be mindful of me, O most gracious God! Grant me a safe passage through this vale of sin and sorrow, and, in the true path, conduct me to the heavenly kingdom. Amen. Lord, hear also the prayer in the 47th chapter, and calm my mind, and strengthen me for future duty.

———◦———

July 15, 1827.

To-morrow I begin the first infant school. It is an important period of my life, and I now desire to acknowledge the goodness of God in permitting me to see the work so far. I wished to have others go forward, and then I would have helped, being averse to appear before the public in my widowed state; but the Lord has ordered it otherwise. He has evidently made it my duty to go first in this work; and although the weather is very hot, and flesh and blood shrink from the labor before me, yet I dare not draw back, but go forward trusting, yea, knowing that my

strength shall be equal to my day. Lord, only give
me the consolation of hearing Thee say, "Fear thou
not, for I am with thee; be not dismayed, for I am
thy God: I will strengthen thee; yea, I will help
thee; yea, I will uphold thee with the right hand of
my righteousness."

May all engaged in this new institution have a
single eye to Thy glory. May we go from our knees
to every duty, first asking help of Thee, and then,
believing Thy promise, go forward in the work. It
is, again, the weaker vessels that commence this work,
as they did the Sabbath-school; and we have the
same promises, the same throne of grace, the same
dear, compassionate Savior, the same Holy Spirit to
influence us, and the same Father, who pities us as
His children, and can as well work by few as by
many, by the weak as by the strong, and who, for
His own glory, will bring to pass what we commit to
Him. "That they may see, and know, and consider,
and understand together, that the hand of the Lord
has done this, and the Holy One of Israel hath created it." O may the little one become a thousand; and,
like the Sabbath-schools, may infant schools spread
over the land. Oh, is it not a fulfillment of the prophecies, that out of the mouths of babes and sucklings
the Lord will perfect praise? O Lord, pardon our
sins for so long neglecting these children. O let them
all now be gathered into schools. The silver and the
gold are Thine, as well as the cattle upon a thousand
hills, and the hearts of all men are in Thine hand,

and Thou canst turn them as rivers of waters. Turn, then, the attention of the rich to this work. Counsel our counselors. Give zeal and diligence to our managers; and look in mercy on thy handmaid, who is again at the head of a new institution, and to whom many are looking for advice and instruction on this subject. Bless all the teachers who shall engage in the work. May they indeed be apt to teach, and may our scholars be apt to learn. O take these lambs in Thine arms, and may a numerous seed to serve Thee be furnished by the infant schools. As the garden causeth things that are sown in it to spring forth, so may the Lord cause righteousness and praise to spring forth before all nations. I now commit this work to Thee, O Lord. Give me to the work. I go forth in Thy strength; may it be perfected in my weakness.

New York, Sabbath, August 26th, 1827.

Detained at home by slight indisposition and bad weather. Blessed be God, he is not confined to temples made with hands, but dwelleth with them that are lowly and of a contrite heart. Is my heart a contrite one? Am I meek and lowly, like my Master, whose disciple I profess to be? These are questions which I tremble to answer. I can only say that I aim at being so; but I am like the rebellious children of Israel — when in prosperity I wax fat and kick, but when the Lord sends trouble, and I have

none to go to but to Him, then, literally, when He
slays me, I trust in Him. I feel daily that it is not
in man that walketh to direct his steps; and I feel
and see, more and more, that vain is the help of man,
even the best of them. To whom, then, can I go?
Lord, to Thee only, for Thou only hast the words
of eternal life; to Thee belong the issues of life and
death. In the day of perplexity I will record the
precious words of comfort to which I opened yesterday, when looking for comfort and counsel. The first
I lighted on was Job, v., verse 8 to the end, marked
by my beloved husband's hand April, 1821. Oh how
often do his marks meet my experience, now that I
am left alone to struggle with difficulties. How
meekly did he bear all of them. How often did he
bear the contradictions, not only of sinners, but professed Christians. But now all his trials are over;
he has fought the good fight, and (oh bless the Lord,
O my soul) he rests from his labors, and his works
do follow him. While I am left to walk the same
road, oh that I may follow him as he followed Christ.
"Lord, help me, or I perish," must still be my cry.
Thou seest that I am ready to give up; that I sink
in deep mire, where there is no standing. I walk in
darkness, and have no light. Lord, lift Thou again
the light of Thy reconciled countenance upon me;
and then, notwithstanding all my trials, I shall have
more joy than they whose corn and wine abound.

I would again seek unto God, and unto God would
I commit my cause; which doeth great things, and

and unsearchable, marvelous things without number; who giveth rain unto the earth, and sendeth waters upon the fields, to set up on high those that be low, that those that mourn may be exalted to *safety.*

"He disappointeth the devices of the crafty, so that their hands can not perform their enterprise; but He saveth the poor from the sword, from their mouth, and from the hand of the mighty. So the poor hath hope, and iniquity stoppeth her mouth. Behold, happy is the man whom the Lord correcteth: therefore despise not thou the chastening of the Almighty; for He maketh sore, and bindeth up; He woundeth, and His hands make whole. He shall deliver thee in six troubles; yea, in seven there shall no evil touch thee. In famine, He shall redeem thee from death; and in war, from the power of the sword. Thou shalt be hid from *the scourge of the tongue;* neither shalt thou be afraid of destruction when it cometh. And thou shalt know that thy tabernacle shall be in peace; and thou shalt visit my habitation, and shall not sin. Thou shalt know also that thy seed shall be great, and thine offspring as the grass of the earth. Thou shalt come to thy grave in a full age, like as a shock of corn cometh in in his season. Lo this, we have searched it, so it is; hear it, and know thou it for thy good."

O Lord, I record these precious passages given for the comfort of Thy servant of old, and left on record for the comfort of Thy people in every age. I desire to believe that Thou wilt again show me the

way wherein I should walk; that, although I know
not now, yet I shall hereafter, wherefore Thou con-
tendest with me; that, when this affliction has answered the purpose for which it was sent, that Thou
wilt give me the victory over all my enemies, spiritual and temporal. I have often said, and now again
confess, that, shouldst Thou take all my comforts
away, Thou canst do me no wrong. I do not deserve the least of Thy mercies; yet, for Thine own
name's sake, deliver Thine own handmaid in this day
of perplexity; that the heathen that are left round
about us may see and know that it is no vain thing
to serve the Lord, and that the seed of Thy servant
now with Thee in glory are of the seed which the
Lord hath blessed; that, when the wicked would
enter the field of the fatherless, "their Redeemer is
mighty, and will plead their cause." Plead our cause,
O Lord, and "establish the border of the widow."
O let the memory of my beloved husband be precious in Thy sight, and Thy kind, protecting care of
his widow and fatherless family encourage many to
give of their substance to protect Thy cause in the
earth. Lord, remember Thy promise, "He that giveth
to the poor lendeth to the Lord," and "that which
he giveth will He repay him again." "Honor the
Lord with thy substance, and with the first-fruits of
all thine increase; so shall thy barns be filled with
plenty, and thy presses burst forth with new wine."
We have always had plenty, and Thou hast never
yet laid famine upon us. We have ever eaten our

own bread (what the world calls ours), and have owed no man any thing but love. And now I come to Thee, my God, with the same words I went to Thee when first I was left alone—ever Thine own precious promise: "In all thy ways acknowledge God, and He will direct Thy paths." I again commit my way unto Thee, "trusting that Thou wilt bring it to pass." I again cast my burden on the Lord; do Thou sustain it. I again look unto the hills from whence cometh my aid. My safety cometh from the Lord, who made heaven and earth. As the eyes of a servant are unto the hand of his master, and as the eyes of a maiden unto the hand of her mistress, so my eyes wait upon the Lord my God, until He have mercy upon me. Have mercy upon me; O Lord, have mercy upon me, for I am exceedingly filled with contempt. My soul is exceedingly filled with the scorning of those that are at ease, and with the contempt of the proud. Blessed be the Lord, who has not yet given me a prey to their teeth. If it had not been the Lord who was on our side, when men rose up against us, then they had swallowed us up quick, when their wrath was kindled against us. Then, in days that are past, the waters had overwhelmed us, the stream had gone over our soul. Blessed be the Lord (who did not then, and, I trust, will not now), give us a prey to their teeth; but, as our souls escaped, as a bird out of the snares of the fowler—the snares were broken, and we escaped—so, O Lord, may I now escape from the snares laid for me. May my soul

H

escape, and the snare be broken. My help is in the name of the Lord, who made heaven and earth.

The name of the Lord is a strong tower; the righteous runneth into it and are safe. I this day take refuge in that tower. I desire to trust in the Lord, pleading His promise that I shall be as Mount Zion, which can not be removed, but abideth forever; "that, as the mountains are round about Jerusalem, so the Lord is round about His people from henceforth, even forever;" for the rod of the wicked shall not rest upon the righteous, lest the righteous *put forth their hand unto iniquity.* I now leave myself in Thy hands. Guide me with Thy counsel. May I hear a voice behind me, saying, "This is the way; walk ye in it." I record this day that, if the Lord deliver me from the snares laid for me, and disappoint the devices of the crafty — if the Lord will plead the cause of the fatherless, and establish the border of the widow, it will be by His own might alone, and of His own good mercy, and entirely unmerited by me or mine. For His own name's sake will He do it, and *He* only shall have the praise, and shall be honored with the first-fruits of the increase, if increase there be. And if, in His adorable providence, He sees fit to deny my request, and for a time permit the wicked to triumph, I will yet look again unto His holy temple. I leave myself and mine in His hands; let Him do what seemeth Him good; let Him visit our sins with chastisement, and our iniquities with rods; but, if He take not from us His loving-kindness, nor alter the word which He has spoken, and in which *I trust*, all will be well, and He shall have the praise. We shall all rejoice at last— no wanderer lost—a family in heaven.

> "A few more rolling seas, at most,
> Will land me on fair Canaan's coast,
> Where I shall sing my song of grace,
> And see my glorious Hiding-place."

Let me not forget to acknowledge the goodness of God to my beloved son, for whom the Lord has done great things, whereof my heart is glad. All the prayers of his dear father seem now answered, even to "a contented mind." He seems to, and I trust he *does*, lay aside every weight, and the sin that most easily besets him, and run with patience the race set before him. He is now content to take charge of a country congregation, with a small salary. Oh what would I not have given, some years since, for the assurance of what I now see! His dear father was not permitted to see it, although he died in the faith of it. And now it would again seem that, respecting my beloved children, I have not a wish ungratified. The Lord has granted all my petitions, and shall I murmur at the loss of a little yellow dross, and shrink from a trial which only affects worldly property? Nay; rather let me rejoice that I have not my portion in this world. Be with the dear youth this day, heavenly Father; give him to feed Thy flock; make him a workman that needeth not to be ashamed, and give him souls for hire, and make him content with his wages.

This evening is set apart for the ordination of my
beloved son to the ministry of reconciliation; and all
the prayers put up for him by his dear father and
grandmother are about to be answered in the very
spot where his father and I offered him to the Lord
in the sacrament of baptism, devoting him not only
to God as his servant, but, with full purpose of heart,
we, like Hannah, lent him to the Lord all the days
of his life. For this child we prayed; therefore, also,
lent we him to the Lord; as long as he liveth shall
he be lent to the Lord; and now, behold, he worships
the Lord *there*, even in the very spot where the loan
was made, and now the resting-place of the remains
of his dear, dear father and grandmother. He deliv-
ers there his last trial discourse, and passes his last
examination.

My heart rejoiceth in the Lord, my horn is exalted
in the Lord, my mouth is enlarged over mine enemies, because I rejoice in Thy salvation. There is
none holy like the Lord, for there is none beside
Thee, neither is there any rock like our God. Talk
no more so exceeding proudly; let not arrogancy
come out of your mouth, for the Lord is a God of
knowledge, and by Him actions are weighed. The
bands of the mighty men are broken, and they that
stumbled are girded with strength. The Lord kill-
eth and maketh alive; He bringeth down to the
grave and bringeth up. The Lord maketh poor and

maketh rich; He bringeth low and lifteth up; for the pillars of the earth are the Lord's, and he hath set the world upon them. He will keep the feet of His saints, and the wicked shall be silent in darkness, for by strength shall no man prevail. The adversaries of the Lord shall be broken in pieces; out of heaven shall be thunder upon them. The Lord shall judge the ends of the earth; and He shall give strength to His king, and exalt the horn of His anointed. Amen. Even so, Lord Jesus! do as Thou hast said. Thou hast heard and answered all our prayers for this dear son; and although Thou hast permitted me only to view the affecting scene of his ordination on earth, I trust the dear departed will view it from heaven. Happy, happy husband, thou restest from thy labors, and witnessest the answer to thy prayers in thy dear son, and no longer, like thy bereaved widow, strugglest with a body of sin and death. Thou art where the wicked cease from troubling and where the weary are at rest. Happy, happy mother, the mournful days of thy widowhood are over, and so mine will soon be. Oh to be faithful unto death, that I also may receive a crown of life. Lord, look on Thy sinful worm! I am feeble and helpless in myself, insufficient for the numerous duties assigned me in Thy providence, and to struggle against the devices of the wicked and those that would swallow me up. Thou didst carry those dear relatives through their weary pilgrimage—wast their pillar of cloud by day and their pillar of fire by night.

Thou didst guide them by Thy counsel here, and Thou hast now received them to Thy glory. Now be to me as to them. I would not take a step without Thee. O continue to hold me by Thy right hand, and let my enemies see that Thou art still the God of the family of the dear departed saints who trusted in Thee, and see the great goodness which Thou hast laid up for them that fear Thee—which Thou hast wrought for them that trust in Thee before the sons of men, and that we are of the seed which the Lord hast planted. Thou hast completely weaned me from trusting in man. Lover and friend hast Thou put far from me, and my acquaintance in darkness; but the Lord still reigns; blessed be my Rock!

I come now, as I have often before, to devote MY-SELF, *my family*, *my substance*, *my talents* to Thy service. O fulfill Thy gracious promise, that if we acknowledge Thee in all our ways, Thou wilt direct our steps. O let not my enemies triumph over me; hide me from the scourge of the tongue; and oh, set a watch upon my lips, that I offend not with my tongue. Deliver me, Lord, from my besetting sin; and may I see that when my ways please the Lord He will make the very stones to be at peace with me.

Bless my feeble efforts to promote the cause of my dear Redeemer in the different institutions in which I am engaged. Bless, especially, the Infant School Society. Give us, Lord, the means to rescue thousands from being trained up in the road that leads to perdition. O may the time be now come when Thou shalt "teach knowledge and doctrine to them who are drawn from the breasts and weaned from the milk." Why, O Lord, dost Thou honor me in such noble and pleasant work? Lord, Thou knowest all things, and Thou knowest that I love Thee, therefore I love to "feed thy lambs." Bless and fit for the work our teachers. Animate all our managers to diligence in procuring funds, and give favor with those to whom Thou hast intrusted Thy silver and Thy gold. Give us continually our daily bread, strength for present duty, and money for present need, for this and other institutions.

Accompany, O Lord, with Thy blessing, the few Bibles and tracts sent to the West. Look in mercy on my poor agent, who is troubled how to provide a competence for this life, and yet indifferent about making provision for a life to come. Bless the reading of the tracts to him, especially the Life of Colonel Gardiner, which he said he would reserve for himself. I again look to Thee to be with us all this evening. Give to my son George to pass through his exercises acceptably to the Presbytery, and give to Mr. M'Cartee what he shall say to him in his charge; and may believing parents have their hearts encouraged this night to devote their offspring with the same simple, yet strong faith, with which his dear sainted father devoted him. May this be a reviving time to our whole family. Revive Thy work in the hearts of my beloved daughters. Make them faithful to their children. And bless, also, my sons-in-law. Make

them contented with the allotments of Thy providence. Let them feed the flocks of Christ over which
Thou hast placed them, and let them not be given to
change. And oh, my Benjamin, my youngest child
and only son, look upon him in his present responsible situation. Make him all that his father prayed
he should be, and all that Thou wouldst have him to
be as Thy ministering servant. Bless his dear wife.
May she be a help-meet to him; and when the yearn-
ing heart of his mother is cold in the grave, may he
enjoy in Thee a counselor and support in all the trials Thou shalt see fit to send him; for I know that
through much tribulation he (as all Thy people) must
enter the kingdom.

Saturday, October 20th, 1827.

Another great work is done, and the prayers of the
departed saints, the father and grandmother of this
family, answered in the dear youth, the only son of
his mother, and she now a desolate widow. Last
evening George Bethune was ordained a minister of
the Lord Jesus Christ by the laying on the hands of
the Presbytery, as appointed by the Great Head of
the Church, 1 Timothy, iv., 14. O gracious God, man
can do little, nay, man can do nothing, but Thou canst,
and I trust Thou wilt, with the form, give the thing
signified. Let Thy Spirit witness with his spirit that
he is chosen of Thee, and the gift that is in him by
prophecy with the laying on the hands of the Pres-

bytery. O let no man despise his youth, but may he
be an example of the believers in word, in conversation, in charity, in spirit, in faith, in purity; giving
attendance to reading, to explanation, to doctrine.
May he meditate upon these things, give himself
wholly "to them, that his profiting may appear to
all. May he take heed unto himself, and unto the
doctrine, and continue in them, for in doing this he
shall both save himself and them that hear him."
O Lord, hear this my prayer, indited, I trust, by Thy
Spirit, and from Thine own Word. Take this youth
into Thine own hand; carry him to the people who
have chosen him for their pastor "in the fullness of
the blessing of the Gospel of Christ. And may the
God of peace be with him and abide with him."
Amen! Only the Lord establish His Word, and we
shall all rejoice either on earth or in heaven over this
chosen vessel. I would also remember before Thee
the dear brethren, thy servants, who laid their hands
on the head of Thy youthful servant. Lord, reward
those who took part in the exercise, and all who assisted in this labor of love. May their own souls be
comforted and encouraged to devote themselves and
their offspring to Thee, seeing how faithful Thou art
to Thine own promise. O spare their lives to the
people of their charge. Restore to health such as are
weakened in body by reason of their labors. Thy
dear servant, Dr. Knox, O spare him to Thy Church
and his family. Bless the pastor of the church in
Pearl Street; make him eminently useful to that peo-

H 2

ple.   May the memory of the just be blessed there,
and may their memorial encourage others to follow
them as they followed Christ.   As they have now
witnessed the great goodness which Thou hast laid
up for them that fear Thee, which Thou hast wrought
for them that trust in Thee before the sons of men.
My record and my prayer are with Thee, O God of
my salvation, my Father, my Mother, my Husband,
my Savior, my blessed High-Priest, who•art touched
with a feeling of my infirmities, and my Sanctifier!
the blessed Spirit, who comforts me in all my afflictions, whose consolations are neither few nor small.
To the Triune Jehovah be praises now and for evermore.   Amen.

Halleluiah, the Lord God omnipotent reigneth.
Let the earth be glad; yea, let the whole earth be
filled with His glory.

> "Glory to God the Father's name,
>   Who, from our sinful race,
>   Chose out his people to proclaim
>   The honors of Thy grace.
>
> "Glory to God the Son be praise,
>   Who dwelt in humble clay,
>   And, to redeem us from the dead,
>   Gave His own life away.
>
> "Glory to God the Spirit give,
>   From whose almighty power
>   Our souls their heavenly birth derive,
>   And bless the happy hour.
>
> "Glory to God that reigns above,
>   Th' eternal Three in One,
>   Who, by the wonders of His love,
>   Has made His nature known."

February 1st, 1829, my birthday.

I now complete my fifty-ninth year—within one of threescore years, and within thirteen of the age at which my mother took her departure. From my present delicate state of health, I do not expect to attain to her age. My only desire is—which also was hers—that I may be permitted to be useful and active in my Master's service while I live, and not to be laid aside and become a burden to myself and others —but this last I ask with submission; whatever lot my God has assigned me while still in the wilderness, I know His grace will be sufficient, and "as my day, so shall my strength be." I have, in common with my dear mother, often a fearful shrinking at the prospect of the last struggle which shall separate my immortal soul from her companion the body; and I would ask, and have asked my Lord to carry me through the dark valley in the same peaceful, undisturbed manner as He did my dear mother and dear husband.

O Thou Hearer and Answerer of prayer, hear and vouchsafe to grant an answer of peace to my prayer this day. Look upon Thine unworthy dust now before Thee, not as she is in herself, but as one of Thy ransomed ones, by the blood of Thy Son Jesus Christ, my Savior. Through His merits alone I must be saved, and for His merits alone I plead for acceptance with Thee, and the answer of my prayers. Were I to be permitted only to come in my own name, and offer my own good works as an atonement for my sins, I would not dare to lift my face to the place where Thine Honor dwelleth. I can not look with complacency on any thing I have done, for my very best services have been polluted by sin, and my right-eousness I have desired to consider as filthy rags. Neither could I answer for one of ten thousand of my transgressions. These, with my few attempts to honor Thee, I lay at the foot of the Cross, and look to Thee for the salvation of my immortal part, and the resur-rection of my body at the last day, as the purchase, *the dear-bought purchase* of my dear Redeemer. He laid down His life as a ransom for many. Among those, O Lord, grant that my name may be included. He wrought out a perfect righteousness for His peo-ple. O Lord, grant that I may be clothed with that robe. He drank the bitter cup of Thy just indigna-tion for sin. O Lord, grant that I may have, as His purchase, the cup of blessing put into my hand. He conquered death and the grave. O Lord, grant that I may obtain the victory through Him. He passed through the dark valley that He might dispel the gloom, and make the passage safe for His people. O then grant, most merciful God, that when I come to tread the dark valley I may fear no evil, but find Thy rod and Thy staff supporting me, and experience Thy sustaining power, and be enabled to say, "Oh Death, where is thy sting? oh Grave, where is thy victory? The sting of death is sin, and the strength of sin is the law; but thanks be unto God, which

giveth us the victory through our Lord Jesus Christ."
Therefore, my God, Father, Son, and blessed Spirit,
grant that my sins may be atoned for, and my duty
filled by Christ, my Surety, that I may have acceptance with Thee, and that the Holy Spirit may continually take of the things which are Christ's and
show them unto me, and pour into my soul those
consolations which Thy redeemed ones only experience—which the world, with all its enjoyments, can
not give, and which (oh transporting thought) it can
not take away.   Grant, while I remain below, that,
by Thy grace assisting me, I may be steadfast, im-
movable, always abounding in the work of the Lord;
forasmuch as I know, if all be done with a view to
Thy glory, and from life imparted by Thee, my labor shall not be in vain in the Lord.   And when I
shall have accomplished, as an hireling, my day, O
grant that at evening-time it may be light.   When
laid on my death-bed, O do Thou make it; place
under me the everlasting arms, and the eternal God
Himself be my refuge.   O lift upon me in that day
the light of Thy reconciled countenance; let not the
adversary have power to molest me; and, as I have
no mother and no tender husband to smooth my dying pillow, do Thou Thyself be better to me than
mother or father, brother or sister, yea, than husband
—for Thou condescendest to be my Husband—and
may I hear Thy voice, O merciful High-Priest and
Forerunner, saying, "Fear not, I am with thee; be
not dismayed, for I am thy God."

"Do Thou Thyself then stand me by,
And every needful aid supply;
Only to me Thy count'nance show,
I ask no more the journey through."

These requests for my last trying hour I record and leave on the table of Thy covenant this day, when I enter on my sixtieth year. O my Redeemer, I present them in Thy name. Plead for me, and send Thy Holy Spirit to witness with my spirit that I am Thine. Amen. Come, Lord Jesus! come quickly.

Texts chosen this day, with the words of which I pray the Lord to comfort me during the next year, or that part of it I may live, and be permitted to labor in His vineyard: Psalm xxxvii., 23–25; lxxi., 7–9: "The steps of a good man are ordered by the Lord, and he delighteth in his way. Though he fall, he shall not be utterly cast down, for the Lord upholdeth him with His right hand. I have been young, and now am old; yet have I not seen the righteous forsaken, nor his seed begging bread." "I am as a wonder unto many; but Thou art my strong refuge. Let my mouth be filled with Thy praise and with Thy honor all the day. Cast me not off in the time of old age; forsake me not when my strength faileth. O God, Thou hast taught me from my youth, and hitherto I have declared Thy wondrous works. Now also, when I am old and gray-headed, forsake me not." "Hearken unto me, O house of Jacob, and all the remnant of the house of Israel. Even to your old age I am He; and even to hoar hairs will I carry you: I have made, and I will bear; even I will carry you and deliver you." "The righteous shall flourish as the palm-tree; he shall grow like a cedar in Lebanon. Those that he planted in the house of the Lord shall flourish in the courts of our God. They shall bring forth fruit in old age; they shall be fat and flourishing; to show that good and upright is the Lord: He is my Rock, and there is no unrighteousness in Him." "He that dwelleth in the secret place of the Most High shall abide under the shadow of the Almighty. I will say of the Lord, He is my refuge and my fortress—my God; in Him will I trust. Because thou hast made the Lord which is my refuge, even the Most High, thy habitation, there shall no evil befall thee, neither shall any plague come nigh thy dwelling; for He shall give His angels charge over thee to bear thee in all thy ways."

———◆———

New York, February 6th, 1831.

Blessed be God that He has put it into the hearts of some of His servants to make the attempt to reclaim the moral waste at the FIVE POINTS. O Lord, hear and answer the prayers put up by Thy servants for the wretched inhabitants, and fulfill, blessed Redeemer, Thine own saying, when Thou didst dwell in human flesh. Publicans and harlots go into the kingdom, when God has purposes of mercy toward them, before many proud professors and formal hypocrites. But, O my God, bless and further the work of education among the young. Let not race after race be trained to be rods in Thy hand, to visit our neglect upon our children and children's children. May we soon see an edifice rising in that quarter, where all the youth, from the babe to the youth of sixteen, shall be trained up in the nurture and admonition of the Lord, and witness them not departing from it when they are old. Bless the attempts making by Thy servants to restore the wandering and reclaim the vicious. May we, who claim the privilege of being called Thy people, and have professed Thy name, feel that we must accomplish, as an hireling, our day; that we must work while it is day, seeing the night cometh, when no man can work; and may we all ask what Thou wouldst have us to do, and do our work diligently, not as an hireling or a slave, but from love and gratitude to Him who has purchased our freedom with His own life, and fulfilled the law in our stead, that henceforth there might be no condemnation for us. Oh, who that have experienced "the love of God shed abroad in their hearts"—that enjoy "that peace that passes all understanding," and feel "that liberty wherewith Christ makes His people free," dare stand back, and not seek the honor of being employed in advancing the Lord's cause? Why do we not feel more like the man after God's own heart, who would rather have been a door-keeper in the house of his God than dwell in the tents of wickedness? Lord, Thou must work in us to will and to do of Thy good pleasure, or we never will. *Thou must* begin, *Thou must* carry on, and *Thou must* finish every good work. All that we can do is to ask Thee what Thou wouldst have us to do—make the attempt, when Thou hast made the path of duty plain, and plead Thy promise to direct our steps; and, when we have done all that is possible, acknowledge and feel ourselves unprofitable servants. O Lord, rouse us to the work; grant us strength according to our day, and grace according to our need; and suffer me to plead for Thy blessing on the dear orphan family; pardon my late neglect of it. I ought not to be so engrossed with one duty as to neglect another. O Lord, let not my sins be visited upon any of these fatherless and motherless children. Many others have been more faithful than I have been; and may we witness the seed sown in their young hearts springing up, and bringing forth fruit, some sixty and some a hundred fold. Carry on the good work in the hearts of some where Thou appearest to have begun it. Perfect that in the hearts of those who have professed Thy name, and begin it in the hearts of all now under our care; yea, Lord, bless and keep Thy good hand about all who have been under our care—all now, and all that may hereafter be benefited by this charity. Let not the place there be dry, when Thy dew is now descending on all around. Take these lambs, blessed Savior, in Thine arms; carry them in Thy bosom; and, while Thou permittest us, Thine unworthy handmaids, to feed and clothe the perishing body, do Thou, by Thy Word and ordinance, feed their never-dying souls. Bless the superintendents and teachers; make them more faithful than they have been; may they remember that they ought to watch for these souls as those that must give an account. Lord, I desire to read my sin in my punishment in a recent trying circumstance. How many lessons Thou hast given me to cease from man, yet how slow I am to learn! How many broken reeds have given way when I have attempted to lean upon the creature! How many spears of earth have pierced me to the heart!

How hast Thou dried my streams of earthly joy, that I might seek my all in Thee; yea, even dashed in pieces my very broken cisterns, to turn me to the Rock of Ages and the fountain of living waters. Lord, restore Thy wandering sheep. May all Thy providences have a language truly to be understood. "Cease ye from man, whose breath is in his nostrils; for wherein is he to be accounted of?" Fulfill Thy gracious promises to me, O Lord. "Then will I sprinkle clean water upon you, and ye shall be clean; from all your filthiness and from all your idols will I cleanse you. A new heart will I give you, and a new spirit will I put within you, and cause you to walk in my statutes; and ye shall keep my judgments, and do them; and ye shall dwell in the land that I gave to your fathers; and ye shall be my people, and I will be your God." Lord, fulfill the above. Enable me to repent, and do the first works. O make me and my fatherless family Thy people, and do

Thou, indeed, be our God, and what more do we, can we want? Whom have we, in heaven or on earth, that we should desire beside Thee? *None*, Lord. Thou only hast been, and ever will be, the never-failing portion of Thy people, and Thy tender mercies are over all Thy works.

And, O my compassionate Master, at this season of revival in this city, remember, with that love which Thou bearest to Thine own people, the descendants of Thy widowed handmaid. O may these children be made willing, in a day of Thy power, to give Thee their hearts in the morning of their days. May they no longer halt between two opinions, but be determined that, whatever others do, they will serve the Lord.

Lord, forsake me not now, when I am old and gray-headed. I know Thou wilt not. Goodness and mercy have followed me all my life long until now; and through the merits of my dear Savior, who loved me and gave Himself for me, I shall dwell in Thy house for evermore. I trust I can believe and say, "I know that my Redeemer liveth; and though worms shall destroy this body, yet in my flesh I shall see God." "The Lamb that is in the midst of the throne shall lead me, and God Himself shall wipe all tears from my eyes." Amen. Come, Lord Jesus! come quickly.

September 25, 1831.

I must here record the advice of my dear infant scholars in No. 1. Mr. Seton had prepared a lesson and a welcome-home to grandma. I was much affected while they were going through with it. I asked them if they thought grandma was as happy to see them as they seemed to be to see her. Many voices answered in the affirmative. "Why, then, did grandma cry?" One said, "You cried for joy." I told them that people shed tears of joy, pleasure, and sorrow; that my tears partook of all these. I shed tears of joy to see them, and pleasure in hearing them; and, adverting to the commencement of infant schools, I said that I shed tears of sorrow that I had not been more thankful to God for answering my prayers in establishing infant schools, and that I had done so little to promote the glory of that God who had done so much for me. "What" (I asked) "should grandma do now?" "Pray," was the answer. "What should grandma pray for?" After a pause, a boy answered, "You should pray to be more thankful;" a little girl, "Pray that you may be more holy;" another, "That you may be more useful." Thus did the Lord tell me what I should pray for by the mouths of these little ones, rescued from ignorance and vice through our instrumentality. Lord, hear my prayer this night—all that I have asked on my knees and recorded in this book. Make me more *thankful*, more *holy*, more *useful*. May my little remainder of life be spent exclusively in Thy service; and especially give me to train up a seed to serve Thee when my head shall be laid in the dust, and Thy name, and Thine only, shall have the praise. Amen. Come, Lord Jesus! come quickly. Halleluiah! Praise and bless the Lord, O my soul!

Lines suggested by looking at the Portrait of my beloved Husband.

Sad was the day when from my sight
Passed that dear form, my chief delight,
And left me here a lonely one,
No arm of flesh to lean upon.
As falls the ivy with the oak,
When low 'tis laid by woodman's stroke,
So sunk my soul, bereft of thine—
Thy soul of love, that twined with mine.
In vain I stretched from side to side
To find support, which none supplied;
For he who dried the widow's tear
Had left his own sad widow here.

Oh, Divie, I ne'er thought to see
The day when thou wouldst fly from me,
To share in joys I could not share,
And leave me all those ills to bear;
Thou who wert wont to dry my tears,
And on thy bosom hushed my fears;
Thy wife of youth, who shared with thee
Thy lot in wealth and poverty.
No grief hadst thou but it was mine;
No joy had I if 'twas not thine;
Our path in life was rich in love,
With joys of earth, and from above.
We pledged our love to Christ in youth,
And, as first sought, He proved in truth

All that He promised; for secure
We found our bread—our water sure.
Still, hand in hand, we walked along,
And bent the knee, and raised the song
Of praise.   Then joined each Christian plan
To succor wretched, fallen man.

Six lovely babes to us were given;
Three passed before thee into heaven.
Those dear loved ones thou now hast join'd;
Three, with thy widow, left behind.
Thy labors now for us are past;
Dear wearied one, thou'rt now at rest;
And God himself hast dried thy tears,
And given for time eternal years,
While still I plod my lonely way,
No cheering smile to prove a ray
To guide, through this sad wilderness,
Thy widow and thy fatherless.

-------◆-------

October 16th, 1831.

The longer I live, and the more I read my Bible, and witness God's dealings with His people, the more I am convinced that the work must begin with Him. We never will be made willing but in a day of His power.   We never will repent until He opens our eyes to see whom we have offended.   We never will hunger and thirst after righteousness until, like the prodigal, He brings us to see our wretched situation by nature, and makes the greatest dainties of this world to taste like husks and chaff, and prove as insufficient to nourish.   Yet He has promised that "whosoever cometh unto Him He will in no wise cast out." But we must come as poor, and miserable, and blind, and naked, having nothing, and needing every thing; smiting on our breasts, and saying, "God be merciful to me a sinner;" feeling ourselves sinners, we come to claim a Savior. As freely offered, He must be freely accepted, without money, and without price. Nothing will suit our poverty but the gold which He counsels us to buy—gold tried in the fire; nothing our nakedness but the white raiment of His righteousness. Nor can our eyes be opened to see our need till He anoints them with eye-salve, and turns them inward upon our wretched selves.

Blessed be God, as many as He loves He chastens. He stands at the door and knocks; if any man hear His voice, and open the door, He will come in to him, and sup with him. O my covenant God, the God of my fathers, art Thou indeed the God of their succeeding race? Dare I to claim Thee as my God? Lord, I believe; help my unbelief.

These forty years since I professed to believe in Thee Thou hast sustained me, and been my cloud by day and pillar of fire by night. Through fire and through water Thou hast led me, with the dear partner Thou didst give me; and although Thou didst cause men to ride over our heads, and didst even give us the bread of affliction and water of affliction, yet Thy loving kindness Thou didst never take from us, nor alter the word Thou hadst spoken. And now Thou hast brought *him*, and Thou wilt also, in Thine own time, bring *me*, to a wealthy place; and not only me, but all my own children, whose eyes Thou hast opened, and whose souls Thou hast washed in Thine own blood, and made them Thy sons and Thy daughters. Oh, my God, my heart overflows with gratitude to Thee for the unspeakable gift vouchsafed to me and mine. Not one left out; all within the ark of safety, and in a good measure walking in the footsteps of Thy flock. Blessed Shepherd, still guard Thy sheep and Thy lambs. The sheep are gathered, I trust, and Thou hast now begun to gather the lambs. O God, continue to gather them, until not one of my descendants, or the descendants of my dear mother, shall be without.

----&----

September 18, 1833.

The ninth anniversary of my beloved husband's release from sin and sorrow, and the departure of my earthly joys. I returned this day week from Utica, the anniversary of his return to the city for the last time, 11th of September, 1824. I am not yet recovered from a severe attack of bilious fever; my mind much weakened as well as my body. I do not feel able *on my knees*, as on former anniversaries, to confess my numerous sins and shortcomings during the past year, and enumerate the many mercies which the Lord continues to grant me. I bless and magnify His name that this is the first time I have been prevented by sickness from performing this duty. I have been reading the record of former years, and praying over prayers already recorded, and altering, as I prayed, to suit the present time, and my cry is, "Why art thou cast down, O my soul? and why art thou disquieted within me? Hope thou in God, for I shall yet praise Him for the help of His countenance." Blessed be God for these precious words. "I shall yet praise Him." Never before have I been so much inclined to look on the dark side. I have, for several years at least, felt my heart overflow with thankfulness for my remaining mercies; that the pillar and the cloud have been my guide by day and by night, while going up through the wilderness, and that, when the arm of flesh was removed, the Lord Himself supported me. I have often been like to fall, but I have never been utterly cast down. And from spending the hours of this day, the 18th of September, in retirement, with my Maker, who condescends to be my Husband, I have felt greater desire to run the way of His commandments while He granted strength according to my need, and grace according to my day. O that I may be soon enabled to say and experience "God is my refuge and strength, a very *present* help in trouble; therefore will *I* not fear, though the earth be removed, and though the mountains be carried into the midst of the sea. The Lord of Hosts is with *me;* the God of Jacob is my refuge. Selah."

O Lord, Thou knowest, though I can not enumerate them, all my sins and shortcomings during the past year, and also those of my dear children. O, for the sake of the Lamb that was slain, who Himself bare our iniquities, do Thou pardon them, and with His blood blot them from Thy book. Bring to my mind, and pardon my ingratitude for the numerous mercies Thou still continuest to me. And O continue Thy favor, freely offered to all who believe Thy precious promises. Lord, I believe; help my unbelief. Look in mercy on all the families of Thine Handmaid, and suit Thy mercy to their need. Each has her trials. O give grace, and all will be well. Look on Thy servant, the only son of Thy widowed handmaid, now walking in darkness, and seeing no light as to the path of duty; enable him to trust in the Lord, and stay humbly upon his God. Make Thy blessed Word to him, as it has been thousands of times to me, and those now with Thee, who made him the subject of their prayers, "a lamp to his feet, and a light to his path." May he meet with me at a throne of grace at 9 A.M. Do Thou indite our petitions. Incline Thine ear to hear, and answer our prayers. Blessed Master, Thou didst give me a text while sitting in my son's church the Sabbath before I left. Thine own blessed mouth spoke these words, Matthew, xviii., 19: "If two of you shall agree on earth as touching any thing they shall ask, it shall be done for them of my Father which is in heaven." O Lord, may Thy servant and Thine handmaid agree on earth to ask of Thee grace to enable them to "lay aside every weight, and the sin which most easily besets them, and to run with patience the race set before them, looking unto

Jesus, the Author and Finisher of our faith, who, for the joy that was set before Him, endured the cross, despising the shame, and is set down at the right hand of God." I commit myself, and my beloved children, and those connected with them, to Thy care, and make a fresh dedication of myself, my time, my talents, my substance.

> "I praise Thee for all that is past,
> And trust Thee for all that's to come."

If Thou seest fit to grant health and time, may they be used in honoring and serving Thee. If Thou deny me these blessings, may I be enabled to *suffer* Thy will without murmuring. If called to pass over Jordan before another anniversary, may Thy rod and Thy staff support me, and may I fear no evil, and finally dwell with Thee, and those gone before, in Thy house for evermore. Amen.

Sabbath, April 13, 1834. Communion Sabbath.

For the first time in nine months I have been privileged to commemorate the dying love of my Savior. Oh, what has passed over my widowed heart since July 21, 1833. Sickness, severe sickness of body, and consequent debility of both body and mind, and little sympathy from friends. Perhaps, owing to my being so actively engaged in public duties, I have had little time to cultivate friendship with even pious people; and perhaps they have, in their times of sickness and trial, been wounded by my neglect. We are poor, imperfect creatures. If God were to deal with us as we deal with one another, what would become of us? Still I feel *lonely*, but only for the want of Christian communion. As I sat in my pew, I missed the dear faces who formerly united with me in the precious ordinances; not even my Jessy present, confined at home by her own and daughter's sickness. The Lord, however, did not fail to send me a comforting word from the chapter read, John, xx., 15, 16, and 17, especially the 16th verse, where our blessed Lord said to the woman, "*Mary!* She turned herself and said, Rabboni! Master." Oh, how these words thrilled through my heart. Mary was alone. She had no relatives to unite with her in seeking her Master, whom she had seen expire on the cross. He who had so often cheered her, saying, "Daughter, be of good cheer, thy sins are forgiven thee," was no more. All that remained, as she thought, was to take care of the body of her departed Lord. Her weeping eyes could not recognize Him; but when the well-known voice sounded in her ear, how sweet was the recognition. No doubt she prostrated herself before Him, and would have kissed those precious feet she had formerly washed with her tears and wiped with the hairs of her head. When Mr. M'Cartee read the verse, and paused on the word *Mary*, it went to my heart, and I could not help claiming my Savior as much as if he at that moment said *Joanna!* and in the sweet confidence of faith my heart responded "Rabboni, Master!" And during

all the subsequent exercises a feeling of nearness to
Him took the place of regret for absent friends.
Lord, continue to look on me as Thou didst on Mary,
and every trial will be light. I bless Thee that
through all my trials and difficulties I have never
been left to give up my confidence, however cold and
listless I may have been; however discouraged at the
difficulties I have had to encounter, both public and
private, a feeling that my Redeemer cared for me,
and that the Lord Himself upheld me with His arm,
has sustained me. But, O Lord, I am tired of sin-
ning. I am tired of myself, and sometimes feel that
my journey will soon be done. It can not be long
now; but, long or short, may my murmurings be
henceforth hushed, and may I no longer look for
any thing whatever from the creature.

If I regard sin in my heart, Thou wilt not hear my
prayer—and no doubt I sin when my feelings are
wounded by the neglect of friends—neither wilt Thou
answer if I make idols of Thy gifts.

> "Sooner or late the heart must bleed
> That idols entertain."

O, thenceforth may I live entirely to Thee. Whether I eat or drink, or whatsoever I do, I would do all
to Thy glory. To Thee only would I look for sympathy in all my sorrows, knowing that I have "an
High-Priest that can be touched with a feeling of
my infirmities." To Thee henceforth may I look for
wisdom to direct me in all my duties. Make all my
duties plain before me, and be, as Thou hast been in

all the days of my widowhood, my pillar of cloud by day and my pillar of fire by night. Help me, O Lord, to pray and believe, and confidently expect that Thou wilt be with me through the last conflict. O, as Thy presence was with those dear loved ones I now mourn, so may it be with me. Let no gloomy doubts arise; and may it be, I would ask, as easy a dismission; but this with submission. Only support me by Thy rod and Thy staff; place underneath me the everlasting arms, and be Thou Thyself, O eternal God, my refuge, and then all will be well. Take Thou the place, in that hour, of lover and friend— my beloved mother and beloved husband, to whom I had the privilege of ministering. "My dear Divie must close my eyes," said my dear mother; "Joanna will not be able." "Dear Joanna, do not leave me, but comfort me with sweet words," said my departing bosom companion. "Poor *Joanna* is now left alone." That sweet sound no more greets my ear— not one to say it. O then, my Savior, do Thou call me by name. One of my name ministered to Thee on earth, with three Marys. And O, my covenant God, permit me again to plead Thy precious promise, Isa., lix., 21. Only fulfill that precious one to my seed and the seed of my mother; and I leave all other mercies to be given or withheld. Be with all my children and children's children through all the changing scenes of time, and may we rejoice at last, no wanderer lost, a family in heaven. Amen. Come, Lord Jesus! come quickly.

September 18, 1835.

This is the eleventh anniversary of my husband's death. Eleven years of happiness unmingled to him, and of regret for the loss of the best of husbands to me. I renew the dedication made eleven years ago, to my God, of time, talents, and substance—all already His own—but I feel thankful that He enables me to offer willingly back to Him, that He may show me how to use all in the best possible manner to promote His glory, and do good to others, especially in training up a seed to serve Him when I shall have ceased from my labors.

And now, O my covenant God, in view of all these mercies, I come still as a beggar before Thee, and leave the following petitions on the table of Thy covenant:

1. I pray that my heart may be kept humble in this time of prosperity; that, with renewed health and increased means, Thou wouldst give increased desire to use all for Thy glory. That I may still continue frugal in supplying my own and family's temporal wants, and be liberal in advancing the kingdom of God in this world, and in feeding His poor. That I may love the Lord my God with all my heart, with all my soul, with all my mind, and with all my might, and my neighbor as myself. O give counsel how to use Thy gifts so as not to abuse them.

2. I pray that the Lord would renew his work, especially in my own heart, and the hearts of my pro-

fessing children; that He will not permit us to rest satisfied in our present attainments; that He would convince all of us of the necessity of growing in grace, and the knowledge of God our Savior; that our conversation may be without covetousness, and always becoming those who profess not to be their own, but bought with the precious blood of Christ, and bound to glorify Him in all our ways.

3. I pray that all the families of Thy servant and handmaid may acknowledge Thee as the God of their mercies; that the heads of them may be like Abraham, and command their children and households after them, and keep the way of the Lord, to do justice and judgment, that the Lord may bring upon us all the blessings promised to the faithful. That the parents, both fathers and mothers, may be faithful in training up their children in the nurture and admonition of the Lord; that they, in obedience to Thy command, may teach them diligently all Thy commandments and Thy statutes while they sit in the house, and when they walk by the way, when they lie down and when they rise up, and may enforce their instruction by a godly example, never doing that which may lead their children into carelessness and error.

4. I pray that Thou wouldst fulfill Thy gracious promise in Isaiah, xliv., 3: "I will pour water upon him that is thirsty, and floods upon the dry ground; I will pour my Spirit upon thy seed, and my blessing upon thine offspring. And they shall spring up as among the grass, and as willows by the water-courses.

One shall say, I am the Lord's; and another shall call himself by the name of Jacob; and another shall subscribe with his hand unto the Lord, and surname himself by the God of Israel." Gracious God, fulfill these promises to my seed and seed's seed. I pray that Thou wilt pour out a spirit of prayer and supplication upon all of us; that Thou wouldst call every one of the children of Thy servants in early youth, as Thou didst themselves. Hedge them into the right way, and preserve them from the temptations to which they may be exposed; especially bless me, O Lord, in giving them religious instruction on Sabbath. Bless me to ——; may she soon evince a desire to be like Mary, and choose the better part which shall never be taken away.

5. I pray for my dear and only son, that the afflictions with which Thou still continuest to visit him may be sanctified to him and to his partner; that Thy hand may be removed, if consistent with Thy will, and she restored to a measure of health, that she may be a help, and not a hinderance to Thy servant. I pray that he may continue a faithful pastor, and prove all that his dear father prayed he might be, and all Thou wouldst have him to be.

6. I pray for my little household: that Thou wouldst bless Mrs. Wood; may she experience Thy love shed abroad in her heart; may she be a Christian in word and deed. And O, I pray for the poor Hindoo. Lord, have mercy on this poor infatuated creature. What shall I do for him? He will not

mind what I say. Thou alone canst reach his heart. O, then, pluck him as a brand from the burning; take the prey from the strong; and may we yet rejoice over him as one that was lost and is found, as one that was dead and is now alive. Lord, quicken this dead soul, and restore joy to Thy mourners.

7. I pray that Thou wouldst plead the cause of the orphan. Lord, give us the victory in the threatened suit. Whoever he be, may he be led to withdraw it, and leave us in quiet possession of the property which Thy deceased servant bequeathed to them, and grant us wisdom to conduct us through every duty. May faithful and skillful workmen undertake our building, and may the necessary funds be furnished to complete it. Spare all our useful superintendents, teachers, nurses, and matrons to us. Bless the instruction given the children. May they all grow up useful citizens, and be made partakers of Thy grace, and all our Board, and the children whom Thou hast given us, meet at last in heaven.

8. I pray that, shouldst Thou spare me through another year, I may be more faithful to my vows than I ever yet have been; that I may do more good than I have ever done; that I may be more useful than I ever have been to the souls and bodies of my children, my neighbors, and all with whom I may have intercourse; that our Infant School No. 1 may be an eminent means of training up a seed to serve Thee, and that our example may be followed by others, and all the children of this city brought under re-

ligious instruction; that our teachers may be taught of Thee, and that we may have the means of paying them enough to support them.

9. I pray for Thy blessing on all the efforts now making by Thy servants in advancing the kingdom of our dear Redeemer—Bible, Missionary, Tract, Bethel, Education Society; for the poor slaves, that the oppressed may go free; and that Thou wouldst bless the Colonization Society as a means of restoring the poor Africans to their own land, and evangelizing Ethiopia.

10. Bless all in whom I am interested; all who have been kind to me, and forgive those who have been unkind to me. Bless all my friends in England, Scotland, and America. Have mercy on a world lying in wickedness, and hasten the time when the knowledge of the Lord shall cover the earth as the waters cover the sea; and the glory of all will be ascribed to Father, Son, and Holy Ghost. Amen.

And now, O my God, I enter upon the twelfth year of my widowhood. O may Thy blessing rest upon me throughout the year, or that part of it Thou shalt continue me on earth. Hear and answer all the prayers offered and tabled before Thee this day. Bless the exercises in which I have been engaged. Let Thy presence be with me when I leave my room, and go again to fulfill the duties incumbent upon me. And while I remember my dear departed companion, and regret his loss, may I be stimulated to follow his example and that of my dear mother, and finally be carried through my last trying hour, and come off more than conqueror through Him that loved us and gave Himself for us.   Halleluiah! praise ye the Lord.

———◆———

Sabbath, January 24, 1839.

Often did my dear mother say that persons arrived at the age of sixty and over could not take care of themselves.   I thank God I had the privilege of taking care of her; that she had no family cares, and departed in the midst of her children and children's children, her dear Divie, according to her desire and wish, closing her eyes.   Just as the spirit was passing away, a flash of lightning passed through the room, and a distant roll of thunder.   Mrs. Lindsay was near her head, and said, "The Lord's voice, calling home His own."   Oh, it was a lovely death!   How I longed, when contemplating her peaceful clay, to lay me down and pass through the same peaceful death; but there was more work for me to do.   Her last admonition was, "Joanna, you and I have had much to do in charitable societies, and we have both experienced how little good can be effected with old objects; and as you can not engage in all institutions, I would wish you to give yourself cheerfully to the young."   I devoted myself to the work, kneeling by her coffin.   The Lord accepted the dedication, and I had the privilege, shortly after, to establish the first Sunday-school Union in America, the first Sunday-school Depository, and to be, I hope, usefully engaged in Sabbath-schools for fourteen years after her decease. Ten years after her departure, the Lord took from me the desire of my eyes with a stroke; severed the strongest tie, and left me a desolate widow. Often, often she said, "I hope I may not live to see any of my children a widow." She was spared that trial, and from shedding bitter, bitter tears over her dear Divie, who was a faithful son to her, and whom she apparently loved with as much affection as if she had travailed in birth for him. My daughters had married and gone, but while my beloved husband remained I was happy. Happy! oh, never was happiness greater than when the Lord answered our prayers in the salvation of our only son. It was more happiness than falls to the lot of mortals, and it was short-lived. There was even then a worm at the root of my gourd, which I perceived not. The dear head was to be taken away, his work finished. Oh, then again I longed to accompany him. How could I stay behind, the last and the least of the happy trio? But no, he said, "Oh no, my dear, your work is not done yet; the Lord has more for you to do." Alas! I thought I would never work more. Oh how hard it was to be willing to live, and through what fiery trials I passed after the dearest, the best of husbands was laid in the grave!

I have repeatedly devoted myself, soul, body, and estate, to my God, desiring all to be used for His glory; and now I am peculiarly called to trust in Him as my Husband, that He will show me a reason for my present trial. All is at present dark before me; but what He does now, and I know not the reason of, I have His promise I shall know hereafter.

Sabbath, June 12, 1836.

"Bless the Lord, O my soul; and all that is within me, bless and magnify His holy name. Bless the Lord, O my soul, and forget not all His benefits; who forgiveth all thine iniquities; who healeth all thy diseases; who redeemeth thy life from destruction; who crowneth thee with loving-kindness and tender mercies; who satisfieth thy mouth with good things, so that thy youth is renewed like the eagle's." —Psalm ciii., 1–5. Well may I make this my prayer this day, considering all the goodness which God has vouchsafed to me, and the works he honors His unworthy handmaid to take part in. I have experienced both joy and sorrow since my last record in this book. I have parted with a dear Christian friend, Miss Hannah Murray, who has entered her rest, in her 60th year. Of her it may truly be said, "Blessed are the dead that die in the Lord; yea, saith the Spirit, they rest from their labors, and their works do follow them." She was a cheerful, active Christian, amid great bodily weakness. She was Treasurer to the Infant School Society from its commencement to the close of this year and her life. I visited her two days previous to her decease. She was very weak, but evidently knew me. She said, "Stand by you—

Jesus——" I often called her "*my stand-by.*" Her work was done, and well done. O that I may also finish my work, so that it may bring at last upon me the plaudit which, no doubt, will be given to dear Hannah Murray, " Well done, good and faithful servant, enter thou into the joy of thy Lord."

GENESIS, xxviii., 20–22.

" O God of Bethel ! by whose hand
　　Thy people still are fed ;
Who through this weary pilgrimage
　　Hast all our fathers led ;

" Our vows, our prayers, we now present,
　　Before Thy throne of grace ;
God of our fathers, be the God
　　Of their succeeding race.

" Through each perplexing scene of life
　　Our wand'ring footsteps guide ;
Give us each day our daily bread,
　　And raiment fit provide.

" O spread Thy covering wings around
　　Till all our wand'rings cease,
And at our Father's loved abode
　　Our soul's arrive in peace.

" Such blessings from Thy gracious hand
　　Our humble prayers implore,
And Thou shalt be our chosen God,
　　And portion evermore."

The above my dear husband, my dear mother, and the worthy Dr. Morison, now a glorified trio, I united with in singing the evening previous to Morison's sailing for China. This hymn we also sung at Dingwall, at parting with my dear mother and sisters-in-

law, in the year 1801.   Only two of the latter company remain on earth, Miss Bethune and myself, and
only one (the writer) is left of the former.   Oh! of
how many companies who joined in praises and prayers am I the only one left!   Well, my time will come.
I too shall share their joys " when grace has well refined my heart."

> " Cheered by this hope, with patient mind,
> 　　I'll wait Heaven's high decree ;
> 　Till the appointed period come
> 　　When death shall set me free."   Amen.

The last verses my beloved husband wrote:

> " What joy that promised grace imparts—
> 　I'll write my laws within their hearts ;
> 　Engrave them, Lord, most deeply there,
> 　And answer agonizing prayer.

> " I loathe my heart in native guile,
> 　Would cherish that would make me vile ;
> 　Each sinful motion, Lord, remove,
> 　And mould—O mould me to Thy love.

> " I never can enjoy sweet peace
> 　Till inward disobedience cease ;
> 　Till, every sinful idol slain,
> 　Grace holds her sole triumphant reign.

> " Oh how I long to feel the shower,
> 　Sweet signal of Thy Spirit's power ;
> 　With what delight my soul would taste
> 　Thy precious Word's perpetual feast.

> " My heart is panting with desire
> 　For heavenly, holy, kindling fire ;
> 　With warm repentance' smiling pow'r,
> 　While I *myself* for sin abhor.

"Low in the dust, abased in shame,
  Without a single lawful claim,
  I mourn my guilt, yet loudly plead,
  Because Thy thoughts my thoughts exceed.

"Now be Thy hour of mercy, Lord;
  My hope rests wholly in Thy Word.
  Thy Word of promise swelling high,
      [Unfinished.]

Sabbath, September 22, 1839.

This day I have returned to my own little sanctuary, and again heard a most faithful discourse from my young pastor, Mr. Mines, from the third verse of the second chapter of Hebrews. Unexpectedly he gave notice " that a benevolent individual of the congregation proposed taking an infant class on the Sabbath, at her own house, of children between three and seven or eight." Thus I am committed, and I cheerfully enter on the work, trusting that He who inspired the wish may strengthen me, and give grace to fulfill my duty in it. O Thou Lamb of God, who takest away the sins of the world, look upon the lambs who shall assemble under the roof of Thine aged handmaid to receive instruction on Thy holy day. Open the eyes of their understanding to the Scriptures they will be taught, and fulfill Thy gracious promise by them, that " out of the mouths of babes and sucklings Thou wilt perfect praise." O permit me to labor for Thee as long as Thou continuest me on earth. May my last days be my best days, my most useful days; and let me live and die for the cause of that blessed Master whose goodness and mercy have followed me all my life, and who has promised that I shall dwell in his house forever. My prayer is before Thee, O my God; hear Thou it, and answer it for the Redeemer's sake. Amen.

Sabbath, September 29, 1839.

This day I was privileged to begin my infant Sabbath class. I had only three children—Alexander Husted, Julia Dales Mines, and John Flavel Mines, the children of my pastor. O Lord, bless the little instruction given; lay richly to my hand what I shall teach these lambs; and may they, if spared to maturity, teach others, when the head of Thy handmaid is laid in the dust. Give me bodily strength to continue the work, if it be Thy holy will; and let me die in the harness, and the praise shall be Thine. Amen.

Thursday, November 29, 1839—Thanksgiving Day.

This day I have cause of mourning as well as rejoicing. On the one hand, God has permitted me to see the completion of the Orphan Asylum, and to see the chapel opened for religious worship on Tuesday, the 19th instant. Rev. Mr. Richmond read the Episcopal morning service. My son preached from 1 Samuel, ii., 19; a hymn of his composing was sung. Rev. Mr. Van Aken, of Bloomingdale Church, made the long prayer, and the Rev. Dr. Bangs, of the Methodist, pronounced the benediction. All went off well. A very respectable audience attended, and the chapel was more than full. All the children—upward of one hundred and seventy—attended, from the infant in arms; not one sick in the house. Many congratulated me, and asked me if I was not very happy. My answer to all was, "Yes, brimful of happiness." Oh who am I, and what is all my father's house, that the Lord should honor me as he has done? Not one good thing that I desired for this favorite institution has He denied me. For a small moment He hid, as it were, His face; but He has graciously removed the cloud, and it is a time of great prosperity with us. But oh how different are my feelings this day from that day when I said I was brimful of happiness; now I am brimful of sorrow. The very best friend I had, except my own family, now lies a corpse. I went through so much fatigue arranging for the opening of the chapel, and some other society business, that I was completely exhausted in body and mind. My dear friend, Mr. Ward, has for some time been failing in health, and I promised myself much pleasure in spending a good deal of time with him this winter, but on Monday I received a note from Mrs. Francis saying that he was dangerously ill, and yesterday, at half past 11 o'clock, his happy spirit winged its way to the mansions prepared for him by his beloved Master, whom he so faithfully served during the last nine or ten years. The Lord Jesus, when

He shall sit on the throne of His judgment, will hail him as a faithful servant, saying, "I was an hungered, and ye gave me meat; I was naked, and ye clothed me; sick and in prison, and ye visited me." For all this, and more, he did. I was the first person he opened his mind to on the subject of religion, and he has ever been ready to comfort me in all my trials, and to assist me in pecuniary affairs. He was, indeed, always a friend in need; never once refused to give me for my societies or objects of charity.

The day before he departed I spoke to him. He roused from slumber, and, smiling most benignly upon me, said, "Dear Aunt Bethune, I wanted to see you, to tell you I am perfectly happy." I kissed his forehead, and was about to withdraw, when he drew me again to him, and repeated, "I am perfectly happy." I bless the Lord for this favor. He spoke very little to any one else, except Dr. Cutler, his brother-in-law.

And now, O Lord, what shall I say? Dare I murmur that Thou hast taken away my very best friend, and made me to feel indeed alone? Oh, art Thou not weaning me from earth, and preparing me for an inheritance above? Again "breaking my streams of worldly joy, that I may seek my all in Thee?" I trust Thou only takest "the dying lamp away, to bless me with Thine own unclouded day." O may this affliction be sanctified to me, so as to revive my languishing graces, quicken me to greater diligence to make my calling and election sure. O may I sit

loose to the world, and long for the joys of heaven.
And, O my God, look on the bereaved family of Thy
servant, and effect by his death what he was not permitted to see in his life, all his children choosing the
better part, which can not be taken away. O Lord,
they will be surrounded by temptations; do Thou
deliver them, and let not the great riches which they
will enjoy prove snares to them; but may they follow the example of their dear father, and do good
with them, honoring Thee with their substance, and
time, and talents. O Lord, hear and answer the prayers of Thine own people in behalf of this dear afflicted family. And, O my God, let me not forget "to
praise Thee for the many mercies I still enjoy."

Saturday, February 1, 1840.

My birthday, and which completes my threescore
and ten years. I can now say with my mother, "I
have turned the last point, and am now waiting a favorable breeze to shoot into port." I have spent the
day in my room, as it is a most important era of my
life. According to Scripture, I have lived the years
allotted to man, and must now, if I have not before,
daily expect to be called to give an account of my
stewardship. I have, on my knees, reviewed my past
life from childhood to old age, confessed much sin,
both before and since I professed the name of Christ,
but oh, how much more might I confess! But we forget the sins we commit, as well as the mercies we re-

ceive.   When I review my past life, I am amazed at
the goodness and mercy which has followed me from
the cradle, and which I trust shall follow me to the
grave.   I have been reading and praying over passages marked and prayed over by her in my mother's Bible, and reading and praying her prayers in
her provision for passing over Jordan.   Lord, as
Thou didst answer her prayers, so do Thou answer
mine.   Though greatly more faithful to grace received, yet it was not for any righteousness in her,
but for Thy name's sake, that Thou didst grant her
petitions.   Now, O Lord, I would put in my plea for
the same reason, and ask of Thee to hear.   Remember all the prayers I have prayed before Thee this
day, and fulfill all the promises Thou didst enable
me to lay hold of; and O, be with me, as Thou wast
with her and my beloved husband when they passed
over Jordan.   If Thou hast any work for me to do,
O Lord, I am content to stay as long as Thou shalt
see fit; but not a day longer do I wish to remain to
be a cumberer of the ground.   But shouldst Thou
lay me aside, as Thou dost some of Thy people, O
enable me to *suffer* Thy holy will with cheerfulness,
as I trust Thou hast enabled me to do Thy will.
And, O my God, be in a particular manner my Counselor under present difficulties.   My providence in-
dicates that my works are drawing to a close.   Infant School No. 1, the last of nine that were once under my care, will probably close next May, and I
shall have no pleasant work remaining but the dear

Orphan Asylum and my little infant Sabbath-class. But perhaps I shall have my dismission before that time comes. Well, my kind Shepherd, Thou wilt still take care of the lambs as Thou hast, and wilt of the sheep. Oh, when those of us who have been privileged to commence the good work of infant schools shall have ceased from our labors, do Thou carry on the good work throughout this land by others, who shall, with thy Word for their guide, train up infant children in Thy nurture and admonition. And oh, fulfill Thy gracious promise, that when they are old they may not depart from it. O raise up and fit pious teachers for the numerous schools in this city and this land, both during the week and on the Sabbath. I thank Thee for the honor of being at the commencement of both Sabbath and infant schools; and oh, I praise Thee, and would magnify Thy holy name, for the great good that has been effected by both to teachers and scholars. Show me, O Lord, my duty respecting the Orphan Asylum. Ought I not to spend more time there than I do? Thou knowest what is in the way; do Thou remove these difficulties, and make my duty plain.

Thou knowest all things, blessed Master, and Thou knowest that I love Thee, and love to feed Thy lambs. It is not likely that I shall have grandchildren much with me in future, if spared, but look on the orphan I have taken to bring up, and enable me to do my duty to her. Do Thou bless the instruction I shall give her, and the means of grace she will enjoy, and may she be an heir of glory. Amen.

February 26, 1840.

This afternoon Caroline, Jeannette, and Margaretta met me in my room, to commence a little prayer-meeting. Twenty-seven years ago, February 4th, 1813, my dear mother made a record of my two daughters, Jessy and Isabella, going to call on their pastor, Dr. Romeyn, and professing their faith in the Lord Jesus Christ, their Savior—their desire to give themselves to the Lord and to His Church. Now I have full satisfaction in the daughter of one of them doing the same, and have, on my knees, repeated for her and her young companions who shall meet here the prayer of her great-grandmother for her mother and aunt, and which has been answered to them. O may it be answered to my grandchildren. She has long ceased from her labors, and now I am the aged handmaid who am privileged to make a record of God's goodness to my family, and am encouraged to pray for others of my numerous family who, as yet, are without. O Lord, art Thou not fulfilling Thy gracious promise, which Thou hast often comforted me with, "My Word shall not depart out of thy mouth, nor out of the mouth of thy seed or thy seed's seed, from henceforth and forever?"

February 9th, 1840.

This morning Adam Creig, formerly an orphan in the Asylum, now a student of Theology, called and prayed in family worship. He seems to have a good spirit, and I trust will come out a faithful minister. He dates his first serious impressions from the time he was in the Asylum. Says, previous to his leaving, at the age of twelve years, he had committed the four Gospels, and the Shorter Catechism, with proofs. I gave him a line to Mr. Wood, as he wished to visit the Asylum, and begged him to address the children, and pray with them, which I hope he may do. Lord, accept of my poor acknowledgments for this manifestation of Thy goodness to those of us who are anxious for the spiritual welfare of the dear orphans, and may it encourage us to be more zealous, and more engaged in prayer to Thee than we have been in time past. And, O my God, cheer my heart in my loneliness, and remove, if it please Thee, this depression of my spirits; be better to me than husband and children, whom Thou hast put far from me; carry me through the various duties before me this month, public and private. O lift again upon me the light of Thy countenance, and cheer me by the consolations of Thy Holy Spirit. Oh, have I not every thing for life and godliness? then why these melancholy feelings and forebodings? Lord, forgive the sin and answer my prayer, for the dear Redeemer's sake, who can be touched with a feeling of my infirmities, and maketh intercession for me. Amen.

K

Sabbath evening, April 19th, 1840.

"Oh how great is Thy goodness, which Thou hast laid up for them that fear Thee, for them that trust in Thee before the sons of men." Who has witnessed the truth of this text as much as I have? Why, oh why am I so favored above many? Not that I deserve it. My dear husband wrote it on the mantle-piece of the store where he was a clerk, and often adverted to it, and that goodness has followed his family, in answer to his prayers. This day week I recorded a great mercy, a great cause of thankfulness— my dear Margaretta's joining the communion of the Church for the first time, and now I have to record that my dear eldest grandson this day preached his first sermon. Oh, what shall I render to the Lord for all his goodness to me and mine, honoring me now to be called mother by four of his ministering servants? My dear husband and I devoted one son to Him, to be made a minister of the Gospel, and he has given four to our family, all of them workmen that need not be ashamed.

------◇------

February 1, 1841, my birthday.

Not only have I completed my threescore and ten years, but God has added another, and I can not say yet that my strength is labor and sorrow. I feel no diminution of strength, either in body or mind, since my last birthday, and my health is better than it has been for many years.   With the exception of a cold, I have enjoyed uninterrupted health, and been able to attend to the Orphan Asylum; and my little Sabbath-class, except when absent from the city, and when the children have been prevented by stormy weather, has never been once omitted.   And now the Lord, in answer to my earnest prayer, has given me an opportunity of commemorating the instruction He lays to hand, not only to my little class, but by printing them in the Sabbath-school Monitor.   They may be teachers in Sabbath-schools in teaching infant classes.   Thus I am not yet laid aside; but the Lord is still pleased, in answer to my prayer and in faithfulness to His promise, to make me still to bear fruit in old age.   O Lord, I desire to call upon my soul, and all that is within me, to bless and magnify Thy holy name for all Thy exuberant goodness to me during the last year, and during the whole of my unworthy life.   When I review the way in which Thou hast led me, I must set to my seal that, however I have failed in my duty to Thee—and oh, how often I have failed and come short—yet Thou hast never failed me, but fulfilled all Thy gracious promises to me.   I have often trembled and been ready to fall, but Thou hast upheld me by Thy right hand, so that I have not been entirely cast down.   Thou hast given me still a name to live among Thy people, and preserved me and all my professing children from bringing a blot on our profession.   Spots we have, but they are incident to Thy children.   And now, O

Lord, that Thou art pleased still to keep me here, oh let my time be more than ever spent in doing good. Make me yet more useful in the Orphan Asylum, and in writing and publishing lessons. Bless me, also, to my own dear children and children's children. I thank Thee for what Thou hast done for so many of the latter. Carry on the good work where it has already been begun; revive it where it seems to languish. Quicken us all to newness of life; and O, most gracious God, begin a work of grace in all the hearts of my grandchildren.

New York, September 18, 1841, in my own home.

The seventeenth anniversary of my beloved husband's dismission from a world of care, and his entrance into that "rest which remaineth for the people of God." As usual, I spend the day in my room. Blessed be God for the privilege. I have, as I generally do, spent much time on my knees, reviewing the past year—endeavoring to recollect, confess, and plead for the pardon of my many sins and shortcomings. Alas! there are, no doubt, many that I do not remember; but *God* does, and for them I should give an account. I have also been led to pray for the salvation of all my children and children's children, and the revival of religion in the hearts of all that have made a profession of His name. May my prayers enter into the ears of the Lord God of Sabaoth, and bring down showers of blessings upon all their heads. I have also been reading over my experience of former years, and am amazed at the wonderful goodness of God to me and mine, and His faithfulness to His promises. I can scarcely believe what my own hand has written, and think how wonderfully the Lord has vouchsafed to take knowledge of so undeserving a being as I am; and now, this anniversary of the seventeenth departure of my ever-to-be-regretted husband, I am constrained to raise an

EBENEZER,

saying, "Hitherto the Lord helped us;" and, with David, while I sit before the Lord, "Who am I, O Lord God, and what is my house, that Thou hast brought me hitherto? and this was yet a small thing in Thy sight, O Lord God; but Thou hast spoken of Thy servant's house for a great while to come. And is this the manner of man, O Lord God? and what can Thy handmaid say unto Thee? for Thou, Lord God, knowest Thy servant; for Thy Word's sake, and according to Thine own heart, hast Thou done all these great things, to make Thy servant know them." And can I ever doubt again that the Lord will continue to be what He has been, my God and my Guide? No; I must and will believe that He will be my God and my Guide even unto death. I can not now be far from Jordan's flood. Should I live a few months longer I will be as old as my mother was when she departed. Oh that I may die the death of the righteous, and my last end be like hers and my beloved husband's. Lord, I trust that Thou wilt stand by me, as Thou didst by them; make all my bed in my sickness; place underneath me Thine everlasting arms; and Thou Thyself be my refuge, and finally my exceeding great reward." I may have no earthly friend near me, as my blessed husband and mother have gone before, and no child near me, but

> "Thou Thyself will stand me by
> And every needful aid supply."

This was my mother's trust, yet she had children and children's children round her. I endeavor to leave all to that God who has done for me more than I could ask or think. He will do what is right.

Sabbath evening, June 11, 1843.

This day I have again been privileged to commemorate the dying love of my blessed Master and Redeemer, and renew my covenant with Him. About fourteen or fifteen were admitted on confession of their faith. Four adults were baptized—three men and one woman. The exercises were most solemn throughout. My sweet friend, Miss Fox, united with us, and seemed thankful for the privilege. Dr. Potts's subject, all last Sabbath and this, was Philippians, iii., 13. His text was more especially the 13th, though he commented on the preceding verse: "Brethren, I count not myself to have apprehended; but this one thing I do, forgetting the things that are behind, and reaching forth unto those things that are before, I press toward the mark for the prize of the high call-

ing of God in Christ Jesus." All his discourses were
excellent, and seemed to exactly suit my experience
during fifty years that I have been an unworthy professor. Dr. Mason, Dr. Romeyn, Dr. M'Cartee, and
last, dear Mr. Mines, all preached the same doctrines,
and by which I have been fed, though I have not
grown in the Divine life as I ought to have done had
I been more diligent; and now old age is upon me,
and memory so far fails that I carry little away with
me from the sanctuary but the savor of the delightful truths I have been hearing. Oh how thankful I
ought to be to be again under so gifted a pastor. I
am indeed feeding in green pastures, and led by the
quiet waters. It is the same congregation, though
much changed, that my beloved husband and mother
departed from, and most probably I shall finish my
course there. I have little communion with the people, being nearly all strangers except dear Mrs. Coit,
whom the Lord reward for her kindness to the widow. Blessed be the God who has led me and fed me
all my life long, and who has promised to be my God
and my Guide even unto death. My blessed Master,
Thou wilt never leave nor forsake me, though I have
often forsaken Thee. Lord, look on the texts that I
copied for preparing for the holy feast, and fulfill the
gracious promises contained in them to me. O enable me to press toward the mark of my high calling
in Christ Jesus. O Lord, the way has been long and
devious. I can not now be far from Jordan's flood.
Oh, as Thou didst my mother and my ever-to-be-la-

mented husband, lead on my staggering steps the little farther. Is it too much to ask that Thy sensible presence may be with me, as with them, all the way through the dark valley? Lord, though my life has not, like theirs, been the path of the just, shining more and more to the perfect day, yet grant that my latter end may be, like theirs, *peace.* Thou only knowest whether I shall see another communion season. Then, Lord, assist me by Thy grace to improve that I have now enjoyed, that the savor of it may cheer my dying hour. Blessed Comforter, promised by my dear Master, take of the things which are His, and show them unto me. Oh,

> "Let me no longer live at this poor dying rate,
> My love to Him so cold, and His to me so great."

And as to temporals, which so distract me, I can only cast my burden on the Lord, for He only can sustain, and continue to pray that Thou wouldst make plain paths for our feet. Only show us the path of duty, and, by the aid of Thy grace and strength, we will endeavor to walk therein. My prayer is before Thee, O Lord; forsake not the work of Thy hands. I leave my children and children's children with Thee, to give or to withhold temporal blessings; but oh, I can not let Thee go, but would wrestle with Thee until Thou grant spiritual blessings. Though separated from each other on earth, may we all, I and the children whom Thou hast given me, rejoice with Thee at last, no wanderer lost.

"A family in heaven!" Let this delightful thought

and hope cheer me under present perplexities. Amen. Come, Lord Jesus! come quickly.

———⋄———

Thursday, October 3d, 1844.

The Rev. James W. Alexander, D.D., was installed over the Duane Street Church. His aged father preached the sermon, and an excellent one it was, from 2 Timothy, ii., 15: "Study to show thyself approved unto God, a workman that needeth not to be ashamed, rightly dividing the word of truth:" well did he describe what a pastor ought to be. Dr. Potts gave the charge to the minister. It seemed hard to hear our former pastor, as it were, giving us over into the hands of another. I enjoyed that part less than the rest of the exercises. Dr. Krebs gave the charge to the congregation: the burden of it was asking their prayers for the pastor elect, and for all ministers. Ministers are but men, but we are too apt to think they ought to be more than men. If we are fed and comforted by them, we are apt to make idols of them, and forget that, though the treasure is in an earthen vessel, it is still God's, and he giveth to the faithful preacher the food to feed his flock.

———⋄———

Sabbath, October 6th, 1844.

Another new era in my long life. Our new pastor preached this day for the first time to this people over whom the Lord has set him. His text in the morn-

K 2

ing was Psalm li., 12th and 13th verses: "Restore unto me the joy of Thy salvation, and uphold me with Thy free Spirit; then will I teach transgressors Thy ways, and sinners shall be converted unto Thee." He seemed to feel greatly the great responsibility he had assumed, and from his whole discourse I should think he felt himself entirely dependent on God. I thought there was rather a melancholy feeling and thinking who was sufficient for such a work. He began by describing the joy the Christian first felt when converted, and the dreadful feeling when God, in anger, took it away; especially when, as in David's case, in anger for great sin. That no one could teach others so as to see them converted to God unless that joy was restored, etc., etc. In the afternoon he illustrated the 16th, 17th, 18th, and 19th verses of the 11th chapter of the Gospel of Matthew. It was, indeed, "a feast of fat things, of wine on the lees well refined." And thus the Lord has again answered my prayers, and given me a pastor, I trust, to feed and comfort me during the closing years, months, or days of my long life. O may this change result in a revival of the languishing graces of the people, and, O my blessed Master, revive my languishing graces. At evening time may it be light in my soul. O gracious God, restore unto *me* the joy of Thy salvation. O Lord, bless pastor and people, and incline his heart, and the hearts of some of them, to think of the solitary widow, and make my little dwelling once more to rejoice with the sound of prayer and praise.

Bless my Sabbath class; I thank Thee for strength to continue it. Bless me to my domestics; I thank Thee for them. Bless me to the Orphan Asylum; bring us out of difficulties there. O give me those whose sole desire is to train up a seed to serve Thee, and not to aggrandize themselves. Restore peace among those employed as superintendents and teachers; and, O Lord, raise up and give wisdom to those who shall take charge of the Institution when my head and the head of Mrs. H. are at rest. Incline the hearts of those whom I address on behalf of the Institution to give us the means necessary for the health and comfort of Thy family, the fatherless. And now I again go forward in the strength of the food I have this day received. Go with me; set a watch on my lips; enable me to conquer every sin; and that which so easily besets me, Lord, Thou knowest. Again accept Thine own time, talent, and substance, and teach me to use them for Thee, for without Thee I can do nothing—no, not so much as think a good thought; but I can do all Thou hast given me to do through Christ Jesus strengthening me. Yea, Lord, enable me to say, "I will go in the strength of the Lord God; I will make mention of Thy righteousness, even of Thine only. O God, Thou hast taught me from my youth, and hitherto I have declared Thy wondrous works. Now also, when I am old and gray-headed, O God, forsake me not, until I have showed Thy strength unto this generation."

December 12th, 1844.   Thanksgiving day.

Dr. Alexander read the 103d Psalm, and took for his text the 1st verse of the 107th Psalm: "O give thanks unto the Lord, for he is good; for his mercy endureth forever." It was an excellent, instructive discourse. He enumerated the causes of thankfulness we had as a nation, as members of the state, as a congregation, and as individuals. He alluded to bereavements in the Church, but said still there were causes of thankfulness that we had the hope of meeting where there would be no separation. He also alluded to the custom, which he thought very proper, of family meetings; slightly alluded to his own situation, at a distance from his father's house.

Here am I alone, not one to sit down to dinner with me; yet, amid trials and difficulties, I can enumerate many causes of thankfulness. All our families are preserved in life and a measure of health; no breach has been made in any of them; all the heads and seven of the younger ones professors, and, we have reason to hope, possessors of religion; none likely to disgrace us; my beloved son, both my sons-in-law, and my grandson, George Duffield, useful in the Church, and granddaughters Sunday-school teachers and tract distributors; Bethune M'Cartee a medical missionary in China, where I trust he will be useful to the souls and bodies of that benighted people. Surely these are great causes of thankfulness, and ought to call forth "thanks unto the Lord, for He is good, for His mercy endureth forever."

————◆————

Sabbath, 29th Dec., 1844, the last Sabbath of the year.

Dr. Alexander preached from the "grain of mustard-seed." It was an admirable rousing discourse. I felt a little heavy during the first part, having no one to help me in my Sabbath class; but no one could help being roused up when, after speaking of seed sown generations ago, he alluded to some lying long dormant, yet springing up and yielding abundant fruit in the same place; and said that one time there was little or no religion in Virginia, when a man (I forget his name) had Luther on the Galatians, and had meetings, and read the book to the people, and it was the beginning of a revival or awakening which has continued to this day. He showed it to be the duty of every one to sow the seed, and to hope and trust that it would not return void. Some persons do nothing but croak and moan over the low state of religion; but we must not only sow the seed, but must *hope* and believe that it eventually will prove successful in some. He addressed us all in the church, officers, parents, heads of families, tract distributors, teachers of schools and Sabbath-school teachers, all, all he called upon to be up and doing. May the close of the year be a beginning of days to our Church; and may we see a revival the coming year, such as some of us saw more than twenty years ago. Lord,

here am I, send me; show me what I can do.   I
thank Thee that Thou still givest me strength of
body and mind to keep up my Sabbath class and visit
the Orphan Asylum; but still, if I can do more, show
it me, blessed Master.   I would like to have an evening prayer-meeting in my house or family.   If that
can not be, is it my duty to try to get up a female
prayer-meeting?   Lord, I ask of Thee, is it my duty?
and if it be, do Thou direct, and make the path of
duty plain.   May my pastor show me how I may accomplish something toward reviving Thy love in the
hearts of the people of Duane Street Church.   O the
prayers that are before Thy throne for that church!
Did not Thy dear handmaid, my mother, spend her
last praying breath in it, praying there for her seed,
and her seed's seed, and the prosperity of Thy Zion?
Did not Thy dear servant, an officer there, visit sick
and dying beds there? and did he not see fruit there?
Did not many weep over his cold remains, and say,
"There lies my best friend?"   Did not my mother
and my blessed husband depart from that congregation? and were not their funeral sermons preached
there?   And did not my husband tell me to tell his
brethren to sing the Psalm, as expressive of his dying
exercise,

> "I'll praise my Maker while I've breath,
> And when my voice is lost in death,
>   Praise shall employ my nobler powers?"

And now that God, in His providence, has brought
me back to it, and it is likely to be my last remove,

shall I not pray for the peace of this Jerusalem, where my mother and husband were comforted in death; where my daughters were born into the kingdom, and where my beloved son was trained for it? Oh, if I forget thee, may my right hand forget her cunning. Show me then, blessed Master, how I may yet bring forth fruit on the topmost bough, and promote the revival of our languishing graces in the Church. My prayer is before Thee, O Lord. I wait for Thy answer. Come, Lord Jesus! come quickly. Amen.

January 5, 1845.

O Lord, I would thank Thee for my beloved son. Reward him, O Lord, for his dutiful and affectionate conduct to his aged mother. Truly he does not despise her when she is old, but grows more and more affectionate and grateful to me the less I can do to help him. And, O Lord, I would also thank Thee for all my children and children's children who have professed the name of Christ; that they have been, in some degree, faithful to their vows, and that they have been restrained by Thy grace from bringing any scandal on their profession. O, gracious God, continue to keep Thy hand about us all, and may those who are yet in the outer sanctuary have Thy sceptre extended to them, and let there not be one of my seed or seed's seed wanting in the day when Thou makest up Thy jewels. Remember their dear father's prayer: "Of them, in every age, may it be said,

These are they which bring the sacrifices of praise
unto the house of the Lord."

Bless my dear old friend, Mrs. Lindsay. O carry
her in Thy arms through the dark valley, and whis-
per peace to her dying spirit, as Thou didst carry her
friends through, my dear mother and husband. She
told me that when her husband heard of his death he
exclaimed, "Help, Lord, for the godly man ceaseth!"
She is the last of my intimate friends whom I knew
in Cedar Street Church (Dr. M.'s). "Lover and
friend Thou hast put far from me, and my acquaintance in darkness." If I dare, I would wish to join
them. Lord, give me grace to say, "All the days of
my appointed time will I wait till my change come."

Bless my instructions in the Sabbath class. I thank
Thee for fruit there. May I see yet more; and when
my head is at rest in the grave, may the seed spring
up and bear fruit.

January 26th, 1845.

O my God, give me fruit in my Sabbath class. I
thank Thee for strength of body to continue it. Bless
also the boy Pye, in Dr. Ferris's church, and bless John
Scott, who has been so long in the Asylum, and is
now about to leave it. Lord, may he be a subject of
grace; and keep Thy hand about dear Richmond
Morse, and carry on the good work which I trust has
been begun in his young heart. Lord, aid me in preparing the children for the anniversary; show me

what my duty is; set a watch upon my lips, that I offend not with my tongue; yet give me courage to do my duty, and show boldly what I see to be the duty of the Board.   Lord, forsake me not at this trying time.   I leave this heavy burden upon Thee, my compassionate Master, Thou who didst bear the contradiction of sinners.   And O teach Miss —— to be prudent, and be more anxious to keep peace, if she can not make it.

> "May the clouds I so much dread
> Be big with mercy, and so break
> In blessings on our head."

Amen.

Saturday, 1st of February, 1845, my birthday.

This day completes my seventy-fifth year, three years more than my blessed mother saw.   As for my father, he was cut down in the bloom of life. My grandfather, who died at that age, was in second childhood for a year, having had three attacks of apoplexy.   And here am I, with all my faculties apparently unimpaired, except my memory, which only obliges me to keep memorandums.   Blessed be God for all his loving-kindness to me, however undeserving; truly may I say, "Goodness and mercy have followed me all my life;" and may I not trust my God that I shall dwell in His house forevermore? My forefathers trusted in Thee, O Lord; they trusted, and Thou didst deliver them.   They trusted in Thee, and were not confounded.   But it would seem now that I am no longer thought of by some who have known me comparatively but for a short time, old friends having been removed either by death or distance. I have not one left in the Board with whom I can take sweet counsel, as in former times. My beloved mother, dear Mrs. Hoffman, Mrs. Startin, Mrs. Sadler, Miss Ogden, Miss Onderdonk, and last, and certainly not least, my still beloved friend Miss Donaldson, who always helped me, particularly at this season, when preparing for the anniversary. Gracious God, Thou wilt never leave me nor forsake me. Let them with whom I associate not laugh me to scorn, but may they see that "Thou hast delivered me because I delighted in Thee;" Thou art He that took me out of the womb; Thou didst make me to hope when I was on my mother's breast; I was cast on Thee (by her) from the womb. "Be not, then, far from me, O Lord; for trouble is near, and there is none to help." My aged associate being absent leaves more upon me in the Asylum. Lord, look on this Institution, which thine own hand planted, and which has been a blessing to many, and forsake us not when we are old and gray-headed.

How often have I devoted to Thee time, talents, and substance! I now renew the dedication, though little remains of either. I am too old, and time too short, to accomplish much, but still may there be fruit on the topmost bough. My eyes are still, as in former troubles, unto Thee, O Thou that dwellest in the heavens. Behold, as the eyes of servants look unto

the hand of their masters, and as the eyes of a maiden
unto the hand of her mistress, so my eyes wait upon
God, until that He have mercy upon us in the Orphan Asylum.

Gracious God, pardon all the sins of the past year;
and as the outward man decays, may the inward man
be renewed day by day.   Lord, hear; Lord, answer,
and defer not.   I ask,

> "In the last distressing hour,
>   Do Thou display delivering power.
>   The mount of danger is the place
>   Where oft we see surprising grace."

Amen.   Do as Thou hast said.

———◆———

April 27, Sabbath.

Dr. Alexander mentioned Robert Haldane. My
beloved husband and I knew him well, and often
united with him in prayer for the spread of the Word
of God.   My dear companion was a perfect Concord-
ance; could give chapter and verse when he quoted
Scripture.   When I was going to read my mother's
provision for passing Jordan when he was passing
away, he said, "No, take the Bible itself; read the
14th of John's Gospel."   While turning it up, he said,
"The Bible! the Bible! no tongue can tell what the
Bible has been to me."   And, after twenty years'
more experience, I can say the same.

———◆———

Philadelphia, November 2, 1845, Sabbath.

This day my beloved son preached from the 20th and 21st verses of the Epistle of Jude. He had only a skeleton, having been prevented from writing out his sermon by the illness of his brother-in-law. He was much troubled before he went because he thought himself so ill prepared. I told him the Lord would bless him, and He certainly did, for he never preached the Gospel more fully, or with apparently more Divine wisdom. When he remarked that the babes in Christ must be fed with milk, but that the more advanced Christians, having to labor and to be growing in usefulness, must have, necessarily, stronger and more nourishing food, a tender thought crossed my mind, that the Lord, in answer to my husband's prayers and my own, had given me to be fed with strong meat by him whom I had fed with milk, spiritual and temporal—the latter from my own breast; and I was much affected, as must have been observed by several. I now record my thankfulness to the prayer-hearing and prayer-answering God; He who leads His people to pray for what He designs to bestow.

I have been much gratified by my present visit, witnessing an evident improvement and growth in the Divine life of my son. Bless the Lord, O my soul; and all that is within me, bless and magnify His holy name. O let me be thankful for apparently the full answer to my dear husband's prayers for his beloved son forty years ago, and may I profit by his preaching this day.

Sabbath, Jan. 4, 1846.

Heard Dr. Alexander in the forenoon; his text was from the 136th Psalm, 1st verse: "O give thanks unto the Lord, for His mercy endureth forever." He alluded to many causes of thankfulness as a Church, now that we had completed one year from beginning to end; said the Session were going to visit through the congregation, that they might become acquainted with the members; that he, as pastor, was going to commence his pastoral visits with the year. I rejoice that he seems to be happy among us. Long, long may the Lord spare him to us. As for me, my time is fast drawing to a close. Oh, at evening time may it be light, and may this dear servant of God comfort me while passing through the dark valley. Amid many trials and difficulties in worldly matters, I have to record an event which, while it rejoiced my heart, caused tears of gratitude to flow. Who am I, O Lord? and all my father's house, that Thou shouldst honor me thus? This day, at my Sabbath class, Alexander Husted said to me, "I mean to begin the year by serving the Lord." How it thrilled through my heart to hear him say so. He was the first that entered my class September, 1839, and he has steadily attended it ever since, when well, and when I have been in the city. I have never needed to send for the children: they always are ready to return, and have ever taken pleasure in the exercise. He makes the third who have become Christians—I trust not the last. He will unite with the Church next Sabbath. My heart yearns over one I can not help considering my spiritual child. Lord, keep Thy hand about him, and, should he be a suitable one to become a minister, provide the means for his education.

———◇———

August 30, 1846.

Dr. Alexander this afternoon preached from the 67th verse of the 119th Psalm: "Before I was afflicted I went astray; but now have I kept Thy word;" a most instructing and comforting discourse, and suited the experience of my long life. May God bless it to those of our congregation, of whom there are not a few, now in deep affliction. I am not one who has not seen affliction, and I may read my sin in my punishment in some of my afflictions. Lord, give me the sanctified use of them all. In all much mercy has been mine. Only do Thou, gracious God, bring all my family within the bounds of Thy covenant, and I put a blank into Thy hands as to worldly blessings.

———◇———

September 6, 1846.

In the afternoon we had a most rousing discourse from Rev. Dr. Plummer, of Virginia. He had no notes or written sermon. His delivery is very unlike our dear pastor, but his matter was most excellent, and it must be a hard heart that could be unmoved under it. His text was Hebrews, vii., 25: "Wherefore He is able to save them unto the uttermost that come unto God by Him (Jesus), seeing He ever liveth to make intercession for them." May the Lord bless it to his hearers. None need despair who heard him. He had many tender expressions; many of them floating in my memory, though I can not set them down, something like the following: Jesus, in His agony on the cross, while His mother was before Him, and others dear to Him, attended only to the dying thief, who "called on Him to remember him when He came to His kingdom." Jesus replied, while the blood was trickling from His side to save him, "This day thou shalt be with me in Paradise." He said many of the Lord's chosen ones were from the greatest sinners; Abraham, who was called the father of the faithful, was, as well as his father, an idolator. Jesus himself chose His disciples from those who had the least appearance of religion, fishermen, publicans. When Peter denied his Master with cursing and swearing, it showed his early habit; yet his Master, knowing his contrition, told the woman to tell His disciples that He was risen, and said, "*and Peter:*" poor Peter, whom he seemed to mention particularly. Paul, too, was another desperately wicked character; yet, when Christ called him, he immediately acknowledged Him and believed in Him.

This afternoon Dr. Alexander dispensed the communion. I hope it was a good time. He told us of many things we ought to pray for at a communion season, but he gave us very little time. *I do love a long pause.* Oh how many prayers have been answered, put up at such seasons. After service I went to visit good Mr. H., and had an interesting conversation with him. His dear wife, he told me, had her senses to the last. She was an excellent Christian woman, and well served her day and generation. Thus friend after friend departs. I am nearly left alone of all those who labored with me in the societies in years past. Well, my time can not be long; only let my God lift up His countenance upon me, and give me the support He gave my beloved mother and husband, and I am willing to go whenever He sees fit to call me.

September 18, 1846.

The twenty-second anniversary of my beloved husband's entrance on his eternal rest, and of my commencing the lonely and trying life of a widow. I have again, for the twenty-second time, shut my door against company, that I might commune with my God, who condescends to be the Husband of the widow, the Father of the fatherless, the Friend of the stranger—the God who has led me and fed me all my life long, and of whom I can say, "not one word has failed of all that He promised." I have been reading nearly all the exercises of former years, and find that many, very many of the prayers recorded are still suitable to the present day. Many of them have been answered to me and mine; but as long as we are in this vale of tears, we must still meet with trials of our faith; still, on reviewing our past lives, we find much sin and many shortcomings to repent of, and must again return to the fountain opened, and wash and be clean. Gracious God, the God and Father of our blessed Savior, hear the prayer of Thy widowed handmaid for herself and those nearest and dearest to her. O may the time soon come—O may it come before another anniversary—that *all* my children's children may be taught of God. It is a long time since we rejoiced over the second birth of any of the third generation, yet there are several older than their mothers were when they came out from the world, and took the easy yoke of Christ upon them. There are yet six in one family and four in another—precious souls, the seed's seed of Thy dear departed servant, who were the subjects of his prayers, though he never saw them. Yet the promise is the same as when first given: "My Word shall not depart out of thy mouth, nor out of the mouth of thy seed, nor out of the mouth of thy seed's seed, from henceforth and forever." Oh what a promise! Lord, enable Thy widowed handmaid and the parents of these children to pray, and believe that Thou wilt

L

fulfill it to all who are yet without. O may they have the one thing needful, and then we know that what is necessary of temporal blessings Thou wilt not withhold. Look in an especial manner on the youth now staying with me; enable me to do my duty to him, and give me to see him, as I saw his sisters, humbled under a sense of sin, and then rejoicing in the liberty wherewith Christ makes His people free.

February 1, 1847, my birthday.

Seventy-seven years to-day, and five years older than my dear mother was when she departed, and twenty-two and a half older than my ever-to-be-lamented husband was; yet here I am, in better health than I was when younger, and my mind still continues clear, and, except that I can not remember as well as formerly what I hear or what I read, yet when I charge it, and keep memoranda, I seldom neglect my various duties. Lord, make me more thankful for all my mercies, which are many, and submissive to Thy holy will in all the trials and difficulties which press upon me. Hear my prayer in the first five verses of the fifth Psalm, and the 11th and 12th verses. I have much to bless Thy name for since my last birthday. I have enjoyed many spiritual blessings, and have not been disappointed in answers to *all* my prayers, and try to wait patiently for answers to others. I thank Thee, I bless and magnify Thy name, that another of my dear grandchildren has determined that, whatever others do, she will serve the Lord—Jessy M.; Lord, take this lamb into Thine arms, and shelter her in Thy bosom. Lord, if it may be, rebuke her disease, restore her to health, and may she be spared to much usefulness in her day; and, O gracious God, look in mercy on my only remaining impenitent granddaughter and impenitent grandsons. It is high time that at least two of them, who are under my roof, should be anxious for the salvation of their souls, instead of thinking only on what they shall eat and drink, and wherewithal they shall be clothed. Lord, melt, or, rather, take away the stony heart out of their flesh, and give them hearts of flesh. Look especially on Robert, now uncertain what profession he shall choose. He has talents; Lord, give him grace; and may he choose the most honorable of all professions, and we see another of the descendants of those that prayed for their seed and their seed's seed proclaiming Thy Gospel, and promoting the Lord's cause in this wretched world. And now, Lord, I begin another year of my life. Oh how much I have to repent of during the year that I now finish, and all that went before. Lord, I must again apply to that fountain opened for sin and uncleanness, the precious blood of Christ, that cleanseth from all sin. Lord, pardon; Lord, grant me more grace, more patience, more perseverance, more long-suffering—a greater disposition to bear and forbear, when I can do so consistent with my duty. Undertake for Thine unworthy handmaid, whom Thou hast so long honored to be useful to Thy family, the fatherless, and bless Thy still more aged handmaid, Mrs. Hamilton; may her last days be her best days, and at evening time may it be light in both our souls. If Thou sparest me another year, aid me in preparing lessons that may be useful in training up a seed to serve Thee when my body shall be at rest in the grave, and I have taken possession of the mansion my blessed Master has, I humbly hope, prepared for me.

<hr />

March 26, 1847.

This evening was the time appointed to commence a prayer-meeting at my house of a few of the members of Duane Street Church. We sent notices to our neighbors, and our dear pastor promised to open it. The night was uncommonly stormy, and I expected nobody would come. Mr. Lechie, however, came, and our dear pastor; we were within the promise, and we had at least family worship. Dr. Alexander read the 79th Psalm, and commented on it. We then sung a few verses, and he made a very suitable prayer, praying for me and mine earnestly and fully.

May God hear and answer it in every particular. And now the Lord has not only heard, but answered my prayer, and given me the inestimable privilege of having the voice of prayer and praise ascending from my little home. O Lord, pour out on us a spirit of prayer and supplication, and on all who shall address Thy throne from these meetings; and may the answer not tarry, but may we soon witness an outpouring of Thy Holy Spirit on the Church.

May 26, 1847.

Our pastor being absent at the General Assembly, Dr. Potts supplied his pulpit in the forenoon of Sabbath, 23d, preaching from the words, "And to God, the Judge of all, and the spirits of just men made perfect." He said he meant "to take us to heaven." And to heaven, in mind, he took me; for, blessed be God, all whom I love I trust are there. He was very tender; and as I had just heard that my dear old friend, Mrs. Lindsay, was probably about to follow her friends and mine, my tears flowed during nearly all the service. From church I went to see Mrs. Lindsay. She was very much pleased to see me, and appeared and spoke as if she knew she would soon be in heaven; but her mind wandered a great deal, and she was very restless. I read to her the chapter Dr. Potts had spoken from, and many other portions of Scripture—the 14th of John's Gospel, and Psalms; but she dozed a great deal, and when awake her mind wandered, which we regretted. Dr. M'Elroy called in the afternoon, spoke to her, and prayed for her. I remained with her till evening, and spent the greater part of Monday with her. I intended to have seen the last of her; but, as the doctor said it would be but a few hours, and she seemed insensible, I feared it would be too much for me; and, of course, I would have to stay all night, or leave her while alive; accordingly, I took my last look of as dear and kind a friend as I ever had, and returned to my lonely home about ten at night. She departed at three o'clock in the morning of Tuesday, May 25.

> "Happy soul, thy days are ended—
> All thy mourning days below."

Another Christian friend has entered her rest. Mrs. Nexsen, after years of suffering, was buried Sabbath afternoon, when we sung these lines:

> "Part of the flock have cross'd the flood,
> And part are crossing now."

I thought of both friends; Mrs. Nexsen as already across the flood, and Mrs. Lindsay as still in the swellings of Jordan. Blessed be the God and Father of our Lord and Savior, who made the passage safe for His people, so that I trust I can say, "Though I walk through the valley of the shadow of death, I will fear no evil if Thou art with me, and Thy rod and staff comfort me." I ask *one* thing, that Thy sensible presence may be with me, and no distracting or wandering thoughts annoy me. I must not forget Mrs. Lindsay's dying request to my son: "Tell your son from me that the next time he publishes any thing he must print Erskine's sermons on these words: 'Do as Thou hast said.'" She named more than one to whom it was the means of their conversion. She also said, "I will not need my vault any more, and I leave it to you; you may put any one there you choose; perhaps it may help some poor

body." She repeated this twice. On Wednesday afternoon she was conveyed to her long home. Dr.
M'Elroy made an address, enumerating many of her
Christian graces, and spoke highly of her; but the
half was not told. Dr. Knox prayed, and most fer-
vently, for the aged, for which I was thankful, and in
which I joined. My days, I rather think, will be few.

———◦———

Sabbath, June 13, 1847.

Dr. Alexander read the 40th of Isaiah, and took
his text from the 3d verse: "Prepare ye the way of
the Lord." The whole scope of his discourse was the
duty of training the young in the fear of God, and
urging the support and establishing Sunday-schools.
A collection for the American Sabbath-school Union
was taken up, amounting to upward of $600. I at-
tended the Sabbath-school in the afternoon, and heard
an address to the scholars. A young man preached,
and very well too, in the afternoon, from the 1st and
2d verses of the 2d chapter of the 1st Epistle of John,
having read the first chapter as an introduction to
his subject: "My little children, these things write
I unto you," etc. May the Lord bless all the good
seed sown this day in churches and Sunday-schools;
and, O Lord, wilt Thou give me fruit in my own little Sabbath class. Now, when Thou hast put lover
and friend far from me, and even my few remaining
relatives, O comfort, and support, and aid, and direct
me in all my numerous duties and cares. Lord, I am

sick of all earthly dependences; and while I experience that it is not in man to direct his steps, and that vain is all the help of man, even if I had it, which Thou knowest I have not, may I still look to Thee, and believe that Thou wilt never leave nor forsake me, but make plain paths for my feet. Make the path of duty so plain as if I heard a voice behind me saying, "This is the way, walk ye in it." Be with me through the week, and all Thou knowest I have to do. Lead me to a suitable teacher. Give wisdom to our superintendents in the Orphan Asylum. Restore peace in our Board. O may we be more anxious to do all our duties with a single eye to Thy glory, saying less to men and praying more to Thee; acknowledging Thee in all our ways, and then we may trust and experience more than we do that Thou wilt direct our steps. As to temporals, I know Thou wilt give "food and raiment, and therewith may we be content." And, O Lord, preserve to me my reason and my judgment; and O, leave me not in this world to be a burden to myself or others.

Take me home to the mansions prepared for me when I can no longer take care of myself and be useful to others. Keep Thy good hand around the only son of his widowed mother, and all my children and children's children. They are the seed of the righteous; may they all be the followers of those who, through faith and patience, have inherited the promises. Amen.

"Jesus, lover of my soul,
　　Let me to Thy bosom fly,
　While the billows near me roll,
　　While the tempest still is high."

————◆————

August 16, 1847.

O Lord, I thank Thee for the restored health of
my beloved son. Be with him in the good work in
which he is engaged, and may he be a beginning of
saving mercy to the "Thousand Isles." I have often
heard my dear mother speak of the "Thousand Isles
—Mille Isles." Little did she think her grandson,
the son of her beloved D. B., would be the first
to carry the glad tidings of salvation there. Lord,
prosper. I now write and sing these verses as a
prayer. O Lord, grant it. May I experience fully
all that they express.

"In the hour of pain and anguish,
　　In the hour when death draws near,
　Suffer not my heart to languish,
　　Suffer not my soul to fear.
　O refresh me with Thy blessing,
　　O refresh me with Thy grace;
　May Thy mercies, never ceasing,
　　Fit me for Thy dwelling-place.

"When this mortal life is ended,
　　Bid me in Thine arms to rest,
　Till, by angel bands attended,
　　I awake among the bless'd.

"Then, O crown me with Thy blessing,
　　Through the triumphs of Thy grace,

L 2

Then shall praises, never ceasing,
   Echo through Thy dwelling-place.
O refresh me with Thy blessing,
   O refresh me with Thy grace."

THE END.

FRANKLIN SQUARE, NEW YORK, *Dec.* 1862.

Harper & Brothers'
LIST OF NEW BOOKS.

☞ MAILING NOTICE.—HARPER & BROTHERS *will send their Books by Mail, postage free (for any distance in the United States under* 1500 *miles), on receipt of the Price.*

☞ *HARPER'S CATALOGUE may be obtained gratuitously, on application to the Publishers personally, or by letter, inclosing Six Cents in Postage Stamps.*

SPRINGS OF ACTION. By Mrs. C. H. B. RICHARDS. 16mo, Cloth.

LIFE OF KIRWAN. Life and Correspondence of the Late Rev. Nicholas Murray, D.D. Edited by the Rev. S. I. PRIME, D.D. Portrait, 12mo, Cloth.

CHRONICLES OF CARLINGFORD. A Tale. By Mrs. OLIPHANT, Author of "The Life of Edward Irving," "The Last of the Mortimers," "Laird of Norlaw," "Margaret Maitland," &c. 8vo. Paper.

MRS. OLIPHANT'S LIFE OF EDWARD IRVING. The Life of Edward Irving, Minister of the National Scotch Church, London. Illustrated by his Journals and Correspondence. By Mrs. OLIPHANT. Portrait. 8vo, Cloth, $3 00.

MILL ON REPRESENTATIVE GOVERNMENT. Considerations on Representative Government. By JOHN STUART MILL, Author of "A System of Logic." 12mo, Cloth, $1 00; Half Calf, $1 85.

CARLYLE'S FREDERICK THE GREAT. Vol. 3. History of Friedrich II., called Frederick the Great. By THOMAS CARLYLE. Vol. 3, with Portrait and Maps. 12mo, Cloth, $1 25.

THE STUDENT'S HISTORY OF FRANCE. A History of France from the Earliest Times to the Establishment of the Second Empire in 1852. Illustrated by Engravings on Wood. Large 12mo. (Uniform with "The Student's Hume," "The Student's Gibbon," "Smith's Greece," "Liddell's Rome," &c.) Cloth,

HOOKER'S FIRST BOOK IN CHEMISTRY. First Book in Chemistry. For the use of Schools and Families. By WORTHINGTON HOOKER, M.D., Professor of the Theory and Practice of Medicine in Yale College, Author of "The Child's Book of Nature," "Natural History," &c. Illustrated by Engravings. Square 4to, Cloth. (*Nearly Ready.*)

HARASZTHY'S WINE-MAKING, &c. Grape Culture and Wine-Making; Being the Official Report of the Commissioner appointed to investigate the Agriculture of Europe, with especial Reference to the Products of California. By A. HARASZTHY. Maps and Illustrations. 8vo, Cloth. (*Nearly Ready.*)

NORTH AMERICA. By ANTHONY TROLLOPE, Author of "The West Indies and the Spanish Main," "The Three Clerks," "The Struggles of Brown, Jones, and Robinson," "Doctor Thorne," "Framley Parsonage," "The Bertrams," "Castle Richmond," "Orley Farm," &c., &c. Large $12mo, Cloth, 60 cents.

HARPER'S HAND-BOOK FOR TRAVELLERS. Harper's Hand-Book for Travellers in Europe and the East: Being a Guide through France, Belgium, Holland, Germany, Austria, Italy, Sicily, Egypt, Syria, Turkey, Greece, Switzerland, Russia, Denmark, Sweden, Spain, and Great Britain and Ireland. By W. PEMBROKE FETRIDGE. With a Map embracing colored Routes of Travel in the above Countries. Large 12mo, Cloth, $2 75; Leather, $3 00; Half Calf, $3 50; Roan with Tucks, $3 50; Library Edition, Cloth, $3 50; Library Edition, Half Calf, $4 35.

MOTLEY'S UNITED NETHERLANDS. History of the United Netherlands: from the Death of William the Silent to the Synod of Dort. With a full View of the English-Dutch Struggle against Spain, and of the Origin and Destruction of the Spanish Armada. By JOHN LOTHROP MOTLEY, LL.D., D.C.L., Author of "The Rise of the Dutch Republic." 2 vols. 8vo, Cloth, $4 00; Sheep, $4 50; Half Calf, $6 00.

BURTON'S CITY OF THE SAINTS. The City of the Saints; and across the Rocky Mountains to California. By Captain RICHARD F. BURTON, Fellow and Gold Medalist of the Royal Geographical Societies of France and England; H. M. Consul in Africa; Author of "The Lake Regions of Central Africa." With Maps and numerous Illustrations. 8vo, Cloth, $3 00; Sheep, $3 25; Half Calf, $4 00.

LEWES'S STUDIES IN ANIMAL LIFE. Studies in Animal Life. By GEORGE H. LEWES. Illustrations. 12mo, Cloth, 40 cents.

PUBLISHED BY HARPER & BROTHERS,

FRANKLIN SQUARE, New York.

☞ Sent by mail, postage prepaid (for any distance in the United States under 1500 miles), on receipt of the price.

Rev. Dr. Murray's Works.

Letters to Bishop Hughes. By KIRWAN. Revised and Enlarged Edition. 12mo, Cloth, 75 cents.

Romanism at Home. Letters to the Hon. Roger B. Taney, Chief-Justice of the United States. By KIRWAN. 12mo, Cloth, 75 cents.

Men and Things in Europe. Men and Things as I saw them in Europe. By KIRWAN. 12mo, Cloth, 75 cents.

Parish and Other Pencilings. By KIRWAN. 12mo, Cloth, 75 cents.

The Happy Home. By KIRWAN. 16mo, Cloth, 50 cents.

Preachers and Preaching. By KIRWAN. 12mo, Cloth, 75 cents.

American Principles on National Prosperity. A Thanksgiving Sermon preached in the First Presbyterian Church, Elizabethtown, November 23, 1854. By KIRWAN. 8vo, Paper, 10 cents.

Dr. Murray's Dying Legacy. Dying Legacy to the People of his Beloved Charge. By NICHOLAS MURRAY, D.D. Things Unseen and Eternal. 8vo, Cloth, 75 cents.

Life of Rev. Dr. Murray. Memoirs of the Rev. Nicholas Murray, D.D. (Kirwan). By SAMUEL IRENÆUS PRIME, Author of "Travels in Europe and the East," "The Power of Prayer," "The Old White Meeting-House," "Letters from Switzerland," &c., &c. With Portrait on Steel. 12mo, Cloth.

Published by HARPER & BROTHERS,
Franklin Square, New York.

HARPER'S PICTORIAL HISTORY

OF

THE GREAT REBELLION

IN

THE UNITED STATES.

MESSRS. HARPER & BROTHERS will commence immediately the issue in Numbers of a complete HISTORY OF THE REBELLION IN THE UNITED STATES. The work has been for many months in course of preparation by a writer every way qualified for the task.

The INTRODUCTION will contain a clear and succinct account of the Formation of the Confederacy of the States; the Formation and Adoption of the Constitution of the United States, and the Establishment of the National Government; the origin, development, and progress of the doctrines of Nullification and Secession, and the various phases which they assumed until their final culmination in the *Great Rebellion*.

The HISTORY will comprise a full account, drawn from the most authentic sources, of all the Events of the War; the intrigues of the Southern leaders at home and abroad; the gradual defection of one section; the great Uprising of the People for the maintenance of the National Life and Existence; the rapid creation of an immense Army and Navy; and the Battles by Land and Sea.

The ILLUSTRATIONS will comprise Portraits of all those who have borne a prominent part in the struggle; Maps of the different localities; Plans of the leading actions; Views of every scene of interest, and of the most important Battles. These Illustrations are mostly from drawings taken on the spot by artists deputed for that purpose to accompany every division of our Army and Navy.

Every facility at the command of the Publishers has been employed in the preparation and execution of this work; and they confidently believe that it will form the most reliable and valuable history which can be prepared of THE GREAT STRUGGLE FOR THE AMERICAN UNION.

MODE AND TERMS OF PUBLICATION.

The work will be issued in Numbers, each consisting of 24 pages of the size of "*Harper's Weekly*," printed from clear type, upon fine paper, and will probably be completed in about Twenty Numbers.

The Numbers will be issued at intervals of about three weeks. They may be obtained from all Booksellers, Periodical Agents, or directly from the Publishers.

The prices for each Number, which will contain matter equivalent to an ordinary volume, will be Twenty-five Cents.

To Canvassers, and Periodical Agents and News Dealers, liberal discounts will be made from the retail price.

Specimen Numbers will be furnished gratuitously to any person who proposes to engage in the sale of the work, by subscription or otherwise.

For Special Terms, address the Publishers.

HARPER & BROTHERS,

FRANKLIN SQUARE, New York.

"They do honor to American Literature, and would do honor to the Literature of any Country in the World."

THE RISE OF
THE DUTCH REPUBLIC.
A History.

By JOHN LOTHROP MOTLEY.

New Edition. With a Portrait of WILLIAM OF ORANGE. 3 vols. 8vo, Muslin, $6 00; Sheep, $6 75; Half Calf antique, $9 00; Half Calf, extra gilt, $10 50.

We regard this work as the best contribution to modern history that has yet been made by an American.—*Methodist Quarterly Review.*

The "History of the Dutch Republic" is a great gift to us; but the heart and earnestness that beat through all its pages are greater, for they give us most timely inspiration to vindicate the true ideas of our country, and to compose an able history of our own.—*Christian Examiner* (Boston).

This work bears on its face the evidences of scholarship and research. The arrangement is clear and effective; the style energetic, lively, and often brilliant. * * * Mr. Motley's instructive volumes will, we trust, have a circulation commensurate with their interest and value.—*Protestant Episcopal Quarterly Review.*

To the illustration of this most interesting period Mr. Motley has brought the matured powers of a vigorous and brilliant mind, and the abundant fruits of patient and judicious study and deep reflection. The result is, one of the most important contributions to historical literature that have been made in this country.—*North American Review.*

We would conclude this notice by earnestly recommending our readers to procure for themselves this truly great and admirable work, by the production of which the author has conferred no less honor upon his country than he has won praise and fame for himself, and than which, we can assure them, they can find nothing more attractive or interesting within the compass of modern literature. —*Evangelical Review.*

It is not often that we have the pleasure of commending to the attention of the lover of books a work of such extraordinary and unexceptionable excellence as this one.—*Universalist Quarterly Review.*

There are an elevation and a classic polish in these volumes, and a felicity of grouping and of portraiture, which invest the subject with the attractions of a living and stirring episode in the grand historic drama.—*Southern Methodist Quarterly Review.*

The author writes with a genial glow and love of his subject.—*Presbyterian Quarterly Review.*

Mr. Motley is a sturdy Republican and a hearty Protestant. His style is lively and picturesque, and his work is an honor and an important accession to our national literature.—*Church Review.*

Mr. Motley's work is an important one, the result of profound research, sincere convictions, sound principles, and manly sentiments; and even those who are most familiar with the history of the period will find in it a fresh and vivid addition to their previous knowledge. It does honor to American literature, and would do honor to the literature of any country in the world.—*Edinburgh Review.*

A serious chasm in English historical literature has been (by this book) very remarkably filled. * * * A history as complete as industry and genius can make it now lies before us, of the first twenty years of the revolt of the United Provinces. * * * All the essentials of a great writer Mr. Motley eminently possesses. His mind is broad, his industry unwearied. In power of dramatic description no modern historian, except, perhaps, Mr. Carlyle, surpasses him, and in analysis of character he is elaborate and distinct.—*Westminster Review.*

MOTLEY'S RISE OF THE DUTCH REPUBLIC.

Published by HARPER & BROTHERS,

Franklin Square, New York.

Mr. Motley, the American historian of the United Netherlands—we owe him English homage.—LONDON TIMES.

" As interesting as a romance, and as reliable as a proposition of Euclid."

History of
The United Netherlands.

FROM THE DEATH OF WILLIAM THE SILENT TO THE SYNOD OF DORT. WITH A
FULL VIEW OF THE ENGLISH-DUTCH STRUGGLE AGAINST SPAIN, AND
OF THE ORIGIN AND DESTRUCTION OF THE SPANISH
ARMADA.

By JOHN LOTHROP MOTLEY, LL.D., D.C.L.,

Corresponding Member of the Institute of France, Author of "The Rise of the
Dutch Republic."

With Portraits and Map.

2 vols. 8vo, Muslin, $4 00; Sheep, $4 50; Half Calf, $6 00.

Critical Notices.

His living and truthful picture of events.—*Quarterly Review* (London), Jan., 1861.

Fertile as the present age has been in historical works of the highest merit, none of them can be ranked above these volumes in the grand qualities of interest, accuracy, and truth.—*Edinburgh Quarterly Review*, Jan., 1861.

This noble work.—*Westminster Review* (London).

One of the most fascinating as well as important histories of the century.—*Cor. N. Y. Evening Post.*

The careful study of these volumes will infallibly afford a feast both rich and rare.—*Baltimore Republican.*

Already takes a rank among standard works of history.—*London Critic.*

Mr. Motley's prose epic.—*London Spectator.*

Its pages are pregnant with instruction.—*London Literary Gazette.*

We may profit by almost every page of his narrative. All the topics which agitate us now are more or less vividly presented in the History of the United Netherlands.—*New York Times.*

Bears on every page marks of the same vigorous mind that produced "The Rise of the Dutch Republic;" but the new work is riper, mellower, and though equally racy of the soil, softer flavored. The inspiring idea which breathes through Mr. Motley's histories and colors the whole texture of his narrative, is the grandeur of that memorable struggle in the 16th century by which the human mind broke the thraldom of religious intolerance and achieved its independence.—*The World, N. Y.*

The name of Motley now stands in the very front rank of living historians. His *Dutch Republic* took the world by surprise; but the favorable verdict then given is now only the more deliberately confirmed on the publication of the continued story under the title of the *His'ory of the United Netherlands.* All the nerve, and power, and substance of juicy life are there, lending a charm to every page.—*Church Journal, N. Y.*

Motley, indeed, has produced a prose epic, and his fighting scenes are as real, spirited, and life-like as the combats in the Iliad.—*The Press* (Phila.).

His history is as interesting as a romance, and as reliable as a proposition of Euclid. Clio never had a more faithful disciple. We advise every reader whose means will permit to become the owner of these fascinating volumes, assuring him that he will never regret the investment.—*Christian Intelligencer, N. Y.*

Published by HARPER & BROTHERS,
Franklin Square, New York.

☞ HARPER & BROTHERS will send the above Work by Mail, postage pre-paid (for any distance in the United States under 3000 miles), on receipt of the Money.

By Thomas Carlyle.

HISTORY OF FRIEDRICH II. OF PRUSSIA, CALL-
ED FREDERICK THE GREAT. By Thomas
Carlyle. 3 vols. now ready. Portrait, Maps, and
Plans. 12mo, Cloth, $1 25 per volume; Sheep, $1 50
per vol.; Half Calf, $2 10 per vol.

THE FRENCH REVOLUTION. A History. By
Thomas Carlyle. Newly Revised. With Portrait
of Author. 2 vols. 12mo, Cloth, $2 00; Sheep,
$2 50; Half Calf, $3 70.

OLIVER CROMWELL'S LETTERS AND SPEECH-
ES. Including Supplement to the First Edition. With
Elucidations. By Thomas Carlyle. Portraits. 2
vols. 12mo, Cloth, $2 00; Sheep, $2 50; Half Calf,
$3 70.

PAST AND PRESENT, CHARTISM, AND SAR-
TOR RESARTUS. By Thomas Carlyle. New
Edition. One vol. 12mo, Cloth, $1 00; Sheep,
$1 25; Half Calf, $1 85.

Mr. Carlyle is about the only living writer whose opinions are
of value, even when it is impossible to agree with them. No one
is more fond than he of paradox, but few men's paradoxes hint at
so important truths. No one with a more autocratic dogmatism
sets up strong men as heroes, or condemns the hapless possessors
of pot-bellies to infamy; but then his judgments, even where they
can not be confirmed, always enforce some weighty principle which
we were in danger of forgetting. And if it sometimes happens
that neither the hero nor the principles commend themselves, still
the thoroughness of the execution and the fire with which all his
writings are instinct, never fail to make a great work.—*London Review.*

Published by HARPER & BROTHERS,
Franklin Square, N. Y.

CURTIS'S HISTORY

OF THE

CONSTITUTION.

HISTORY OF THE ORIGIN, FORMATION, AND ADOP-
TION OF THE CONSTITUTION OF THE UNITED
STATES. By GEORGE TICKNOR CURTIS. Complete in 2 vols.
8vo, Muslin, $4 00 ; Law Sheep, $5 00 ; Half Calf, $6 00.

A book so thorough as this in the comprehension of its subject, so impartial
in the summing up of its judgments, so well considered in its method, and so
truthful in its matter, may safely challenge the most exhaustive criticism. The
Constitutional History of our country has not before been made the subject of a
special treatise. We may congratulate ourselves that an author has been found
so capable to do full justice to it; for that the work will take its rank among the
received text-books of our political literature will be questioned by no one who
has given it a careful perusal.—*National Intelligencer.*

We know of no person who is better qualified (now that the late Daniel Web-
ster is no more), to undertake this important history.—*Boston Journal.*

It will take its place among the classics of American literature.—*Boston Courier.*

The author has given years to the preliminary studies, and nothing has escaped him in the patient and conscientious researches to which he has devoted
so ample a portion of time. Indeed, the work has been so thoroughly performed
that it will never need to be done over again; for the sources have been exhausted, and the materials put together with so much judgment and artistic skill that
taste and the sense of completeness are entirely satisfied.—*N. Y. Daily Times.*

A most important and valuable contribution to the historical and political literature of the United States. All publicists and students of public law will be
grateful to Mr. Curtis for the diligence and assiduity with which he has wrought
out the great mine of diplomatic lore in which the foundations of the American
Constitution are laid, and for the light he has thrown on his wide and arduous
subject.—*London Morning Chronicle.*

To trace the history of the formation of the Constitution, and explain the circumstances of the time and country out of which its various provisions grew, is a
task worthy of the highest talent. To have performed that task in a satisfacto-
ry manner is an achievement with which an honorable ambition may well be
gratified. We can honestly say that in our opinion Mr. Curtis has fairly won
this distinction.—*N. Y. Courier and Enquirer.*

We have seen no history which surpasses it in the essential qualities of a
standard work destined to hold a permanent place in the impartial judgment of
future generations.—*Boston Traveler.*

Should the second volume sustain the character of the first, we hazard nothing
in claiming for the entire publication the character of a standard work. It will
furnish the only sure guide to the interpretation of the Constitution, by unfolding
historically the wants it was intended to supply, and the evils which it was intended to remedy.—*Boston Daily Advertiser.*

This volume is an important contribution to our constitutional and historical
literature. * * * Every true friend of the Constitution will gladly welcome it.
The author has presented a narrative clear and interesting. It evinces careful
research, skillful handling of material, lucid statement, and a desire to write in
a tone and manner worthy of the great theme.—*Boston Post.*

Published by HARPER & BROTHERS,
Franklin Square, New York.

⁎ HARPER & BROTHERS will send the above Work by Mail, postage paid (for
any distance in the United States under 3000 miles), on receipt of the Money.

THE

LAND AND THE BOOK;

OR,

BIBLICAL ILLUSTRATIONS DRAWN FROM THE MANNERS AND CUSTOMS, THE SCENES AND SCENERY OF THE HOLY LAND.

By W. M. THOMSON, D.D.,

Twenty-five Years a Missionary of the A.B.C.F.M. in Syria and Palestine.

With two elaborate Maps of Palestine, an accurate Plan of Jerusalem, and *several hundred Engravings* representing the Scenery, Topography, and Productions of the Holy Land, and the Costumes, Manners, and Habits of the People. Two elegant Large 12mo Volumes, Muslin, $3 50; Half Calf, $5 20.

The Land of the Bible is part of the Divine Revelation. It bears *testimony* essential to faith, and gives *lessons* invaluable in exposition. Both have been written all over the fair face of Palestine, and deeply graven there by the finger of God in characters of living light. To collect this testimony and popularize these lessons for the biblical student of every age and class is the prominent design of this work. For *twenty-five years* the Author has been permitted to read the Book by the light which the Land sheds upon it; and he now hands over this friendly torch to those who have not been thus favored. In this attempt the pencil has been employed to aid the pen. A large number of pictorial illustrations are introduced, many of them original, and all giving a genuine and true representation of things in the actual Holy Land of the present day. They are not fancy sketches of imaginary scenes thrown in to embellish the page, but pictures of living manners, studies of sacred topography, or exponents of interesting biblical allusions, which will add greatly to the value of the work.

Published by HARPER & BROTHERS,
Franklin Square, New York.

HARPER & BROTHERS will send the above Work by Mail, postage paid, to any part of the United States, on receipt of the Money.

LIDDELL AND SMITH'S

SCHOOL HISTORIES OF

GREECE AND ROME.

DR. SMITH'S HISTORY OF GREECE.

A School History of Greece, from the Earliest Times to the Roman Conquest, with Supplementary Chapters on the History of Literature and Art. By WM. SMITH, LL.D., Classical Examiner in the University of London, and Editor of the "Classical Dictionaries." Revised, with an Appendix, by GEORGE W. GREENE, A.M. Illustrated by 100 Engravings on Wood. (Uniform with "Liddell's Rome" and "The Student's Gibbon.") New Edition. 679 pages, Large 12mo, Muslin, $1 00.

We have much satisfaction in bearing testimony to the excellence of the plan on which Dr. Wm. Smith has proceeded, and the careful, scholar-like manner in which he has carried it out. The great distinctive feature, however, is the chapters on Literature and Art. *This gives it a decided advantage over all previous works of the kind.—Athenæum.*

DEAN LIDDELL'S HISTORY OF ROME.

A School History of Rome, from the Earliest Times to the Establishment of the Empire, with Chapters on the History of Literature and Art. By HENRY G. LIDDELL, D.D., Dean of Christ Church, Oxford. Illustrated by numerous Wood-cuts. (Uniform with "The Student's Gibbon" and "Smith's History of Greece.") 778 pages, Large 12mo, Muslin, $1 00.

This excellent History of Rome, from the pen of one of the most celebrated scholars of the day, *will supersede every other work on the subject.* The volume conforms with the "History of Greece," by Dr. Wm. Smith, in typography, literary method, and illustration.—*John Bull.*

DR. SMITH'S STUDENT'S GIBBON.

The History of the Decline and Fall of the Roman Empire. By EDWARD GIBBON. Abridged. Incorporating the Researches of Recent Commentators. By WILLIAM SMITH, LL.D., Editor of the "Classical Dictionary" and "A Dictionary of Greek and Roman Antiquities." Illustrated by 100 Engravings on Wood. (Uniform with "Liddell's Rome.") 705 pages, Large 12mo, Muslin, $1 00.

Dr. Wm. Smith has drawn up an admirable abridgment of Gibbon's Roman Empire, using, as far as possible, the language of the original, and adopting the plan of omitting or treating briefly circumstances of inferior importance, so that the grand events which have influenced the history of the world may be narrated at length.—*Cambridge Chronicle.*

Published by HARPER & BROTHERS,

Franklin Square, New York.

A HISTORY OF GREECE,

FROM THE EARLIEST PERIOD TO THE CLOSE OF THE GENERA-
TION CONTEMPORARY WITH ALEXANDER THE GREAT.

BY GEORGE GROTE, ESQ.

Vol. XII. contains Portrait, Maps, and Index.   Complete in 12 vols. 12mo,
Muslin, $9 00 ; Sheep, $12 00 ; Half Calf, $15 00.

It is not often that a work of such magnitude is undertaken ; more seldom still
is such a work so perseveringly carried on, and so soon and yet so worthily accomplished.   Mr. Grote has illustrated and invested with an entirely new signifi-
cance a portion of the past history of humanity, which he, perhaps, thinks the most
splendid that has been, and which all allow to have been very splendid.   He has made
great Greeks live again before us, and has enabled us to realize Greek modes of thinking.   He has added a great historical work to the language, taking its place with
other great histories, and yet not like any of them in the special combination of
merits which it exhibits : scholarship and learning such as we have been accustomed to demand only in Germans ; an art of grouping and narration different
from that of Hume, different from that of Gibbon, and yet producing the effect of
sustained charm and pleasure ; a peculiarly keen interest in events of the political
order, and a wide knowledge of the business of politics ; and, finally, harmonizing
all, a spirit of sober philosophical generalization always tending to view facts
collectively in their speculative bearing as well as to record them individually.
It is at once an ample and detailed narrative of the history of Greece, and a lucid
philosophy of Grecian history.—*London Athenæum, March 8, 1856.*

Mr. Grote will be emphatically *the* historian of the people of Greece.—*Dublin
University Magazine.*

The acute intelligence, the discipline, faculty of intellect, and the excellent erudition every one would look for from Mr. Grote ; but they will here also find the
element which harmonizes these, and without which, on such a theme, an orderly
and solid work could not have been written.—*Examiner.*

A work second to that of Gibbon alone in English historical literature.   Mr.
Grote gives the philosophy as well as the facts of history, and it would be difficult
to find an author combining in the same degree the accurate learning of the scholar with the experience of a practical statesman.   The completion of this great
work may well be hailed with some degree of national pride and satisfaction.—
Literary Gazette, March 8, 1856.

The better acquainted any one is with Grecian history, and with the manner in
which that history has heretofore been written, the higher will be his estimation
of this work.   Mr. Grote's familiarity both with the great highways and the ob-
scurest by-paths of Grecian literature and antiquity has seldom been equaled, and
not often approached, in unlearned England ; while those Germans who have ri-
valed it have seldom possessed the quality which eminently characterizes Mr.
Grote, of keeping historical imagination severely under the restraints of evidence.
The great charm of Mr. Grote's history has been throughout the cordial admiration he feels for the people whose acts and fortunes he has to relate. * * We bid
Mr. Grote farewell ; heartily congratulating him on the conclusion of a work which
is a monument of English learning, of English clear-sightedness, and of English
love of freedom and the characters it produces.—*Spectator.*

Endeavor to become acquainted with Mr. Grote, who is engaged on a Greek
History.   I expect a great deal from this production.—NIEBUHR, *the Historian,
to Professor* LIEBER.

The author has now incontestably won for himself the title, not merely of *a*
historian, but of *the* historian of Greece.—*Quarterly Review.*

Mr. Grote is, beyond all question, *the* historian of Greece, unrivaled, so far as
we know, in the erudition and genius with which he has revived the picture of a
distant past, and brought home every part and feature of its history to our intel-
lects and our hearts.—*London Times.*

For becoming dignity of style, unforced adaptation of results to principles, careful verification of theory by fact, and impregnation of fact by theory—for extensive
and well-weighed learning, employed with intelligence and taste, we have seen no
historical work of modern times which we would place above Mr. Grote's history.—*Morning Chronicle.*

HARPER & BROTHERS, PUBLISHERS, FRANKLIN SQUARE, N. Y.

Harper's Catalogue.

A New Descriptive Catalogue of Harper & Brothers' Publications is now ready for distribution, and may be obtained gratuitously on application to the Publishers personally, or by letter inclosing Six Cents in postage stamps. The attention of gentlemen, in town or country, designing to form Libraries or enrich their literary collections, is respectfully invited to this Catalogue, which will be found to comprise a large proportion of the standard and most esteemed works in English Literature—COMPREHENDING MORE THAN TWO THOUSAND VOLUMES—which are offered, in most instances, at less than one half the cost of similar productions in England. To Librarians and others connected with Colleges, Schools, &c., who may not have access to a reliable guide in forming the true estimate of literary productions, it is believed this Catalogue will prove especially valuable as a manual of reference. To prevent disappointment, it is suggested that, whenever books can not be obtained through any bookseller or local agent, applications with remittance should be addressed direct to the Publishers, which will meet with prompt attention.

Made in United States
North Haven, CT
13 February 2023

32509960R00153